THEODORE PARKER

The Critical Theology of
THEODORE PARKER

JOHN   EDWARD   DIRKS

GREENWOOD PRESS, PUBLISHERS
WESTPORT, CONNECTICUT

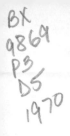

To A. V. D.

PREFACE

THIS ACCOUNT of Theodore Parker's career as a student of critical theology and philosophy of religion is designed to supplement the extensive literature about other aspects of his diversified interests. Biographies and sketches, which emphasize primarily his erudite preaching and his "extravagant" reform ambitions, are numerous. But, the emphasis which has been given in these works to his ministry, his humanitarianism, his crusade against slavery, and his independence will not be stressed here. Our aim is limited to an exposition of Parker's technical philosophy; his characteristic methods in Biblical and historical criticism, his examination of the basis of religious truth, his formation of an "educated" theology and his so-called transcendentalism. Because these are central features of Parker's mind, they shed important light on his relation to the transcendental "temper" in general and to Emerson in particular.

There are many who have contributed to this study of Parker. Professor Herbert W. Schneider has, since the outset of our research, been my patient and faithful guide, and Professor Commager has been a most informed and helpful critic. Dr. Joseph L. Blau assisted in many ways. Professors James Gutmann and Horace L. Friess, also of the Department of Philosophy, have given their generous help. To all of them I express my appreciation for having read the preliminary drafts, for their valuable criticisms, and their constant encouragement. Other members of the Columbia University faculty who criticized my initial draft and suggested revisions are included in this acknowledgment of indebtedness.

My thanks are also due to those who gave me access to the volumes and papers necessary for my research: to Mr. Zoltan Haraszti, Keeper of the Rare Book Collection of the Boston Public Library, who repeatedly opened to me a collection of unpublished letters in his care; to the members of the staff of the Union Theological Seminary Library, the Columbia University Libraries, and the American Unitarian Association; and to the New York Public Library for having located a copy of the rare *Levi Blodgett Letter* which is reprinted in the Appendix of this work.

Grateful acknowledgment is made for permission to quote from *The Collected Works of Theodore Parker*, published by the Beacon Press, and from Octavius Brooks Frothingham, *Transcendentalism in New England*, published by G. P. Putnam's Sons. The Frontispiece is reproduced by courtesy of the American Unitarian Association.

The bibliographical material at the close of this volume is not exhaustive. It indicates where complete bibliographies are printed, and it lists the works essential to a study of Parker's theological and philosophical interests.

J. E. D.

Columbia University
New York, March, 1948

CONTENTS

The Critical Theology of
THEODORE PARKER

Chapter 1

INTRODUCTION

THEODORE PARKER has often been referred to as an important figure in the history of American ideas. His sermons and many of his other writings have been collected and published; many excellent biographical accounts are available.[1] Nevertheless, Parker's importance is said to rest only on his remarkable erudition, his ability as a preacher, and his extravagant efforts toward moral reform. His critical theological endeavors have, heretofore, not assumed a significant place in the study of his career. Yet, this area of interest can best provide us a basis for estimating his intellectual relationship to his contemporaries and the extent to which he took part in the philosophical and theological movements of his day. This volume is therefore to explore the primary aspects of his critical theological views, and, on the basis of this study, to estimate the extent to which Parker embraced New England transcendentalism. Among our central questions are these: What were his characteristic methods and interests? What actually was the intellectual relationship between Parker and Emerson? Which of the tenets of New England transcendentalism did Parker accept, and which of them did he seek to transform? Was he the preacher of a transcendentalist "gospel," or did he at the same time try to keep the more rationalistic faith of the Enlightenment?

[1] See Bibliography, pp. 161–164.

An examination of the secondary sources may suggest
that these are questions which have already been solved.
Parker was, from the outset, associated with the transcendentalist tradition. The terms in which he formulated some
of his ideas and the list of most of his closest associates
inevitably lend support to this assumption. While Weiss'
biography [2] made no attempts at defining Parker's position in American thought, his account of Parker's early
life, ministry and extensive correspondence became the
material upon which Octavius Brooks Frothingham, one of
the first historians of this segment of American ideas, based
his belief that "the preacher" of "the transcendentalist gospel" is Theodore Parker.[3] Believing that transcendentalism's "chief disciples have been clergymen," and that "the
order of mind that was attracted to the ministry was attracted to the transcendental ideas," [4] Frothingham lists
Parker among that clergy along with Schleiermacher,
Fichte, Coleridge, Carlyle, Emerson, Channing, Brownson,
and Alcott. To Boehme and Eckhart are also ascribed positions within transcendentalism, since various superficial
similarities are ascertained by Frothingham. The question
which this list raises is, of course, whether Frothingham is
using the term "transcendentalism" loosely and for that
reason, only, is justified in including Parker. Frothingham
states his justification for enlarging the meaning of transcendentalism to include these names and for emphasizing

[2] John Weiss, *The Life and Correspondence of Theodore Parker* (2
vols., New York, 1864).
[3] Octavius Brooks Frothingham, *Theodore Parker, a Biography* (New
York, 1886), and *Transcendentalism in New England* (New York,
G. P. Putnam's Sons, 1876), pp. 302–321. Quotations are made by permission of the publishers.
[4] Frothingham, *Transcendentalism in New England*, pp. 302–303.

its gospel-like features by outlining its "chief qualifications."

Its cardinal "facts" were few and manageable. Its data were secluded in the recesses of consciousness, out of the reach of scientific investigation, remote from the gaze of vulgar skepticism; esoteric, having about them the charm of a sacred privacy, on which common sense and the critical understanding might not intrude. Its oracles proceeded from a shrine, and were delivered by a priest or priestess, who came forth from an interior holy of holies to utter them, and thus were invested with the air of authority which belongs to exclusive and privileged truths, that revealed themselves to minds of a contemplative cast. It dealt entirely with "divine things," "eternal realities"; supersensible forms of thought; problems that lay out of the reach of observation, such as the essential cause, spiritual laws, the life after death, the essence of the good, the beautiful, the true; the ideal possibilities of the soul; its organ was intuition; its method was introspection; its brightness was inspiration. It possessed the character of indefiniteness and mystery, full of sentiment and suggestion, that fascinates the imagination, and lends itself so easily to acts of contemplation and worship.[5]

Our question is whether these "qualifications," even in their vagueness, apply to Theodore Parker.

Frothingham's portrait of Parker in clerical garb as transcendentalism's preacher emphasized the following traits:

. . . thought and feeling [in the transcendentalists and the mystics] sought the same object in the same region. Piety was a feature of Transcendentalism; it loved devout hymns, music, the glowing language of aspiration, the moods of awe and humility, emblems, symbols, expressions of inarticulate emotion, silence, contemplation, breathings after communion with the Infinite. The poetry of Transcendentalism is religious, with scarcely an

5 *Ibid.*, pp. 303–304.

exception; the most beautiful hymns in our sacred collections, the only deeply impressive hymns, are by transcendental writers.

This was the aspect of Transcendentalism that fascinated Theodore Parker. His intellect was constructed on the English model. His acute observation; his passion for external facts; his faith in statistics; his hunger for information on all external topics of history and politics; his capacity for retaining details of miscellaneous knowledge; his logical method of reasoning; his ability to handle masses of raw mental material, to distribute and classify;—all indicate intellectual power of the English rather than of the German type. . . . Parker was, in many respects, the opposite of a Mystic; he was a realist of the most concrete description. . . . But along with this intellectual quality which he inherited from his father, was an interior, sentimental, devotional quality derived from his mother. The two were never wholly blended. . . . As a rule, the dominion was divided between them: the practical understanding assumed control of all matters pertaining to this world; the higher reason claimed supremacy in all matters of faith. But for the tendency to poetic idealism, which came to him from his mother, Parker might, from the constitution of his mind, have belonged to an opposite school.[6]

We find here several apparent contradictions and a great amount of confusion which raise the question of Parker's relations to transcendentalism more specifically. If the "feature of transcendentalism" which "fascinated Theodore Parker" was a piety expressed in "inarticulate emotion," Frothingham is justified in finding it difficult to account for Parker's intellectual power, his methods of observation and classification, and his logical methods of reasoning. The fact that Parker had "a hunger for information on all external topics of history and politics" appears, certainly, to contradict the inner search to which trans-

[6] *Ibid.*, pp. 304–306.

cendentalism was committed. In any case, we need to know whether this basic contrast existed in transcendentalism or only in Parker.

The importance of this question increases in view of Frothingham's still more positive statement that Parker, "on the religious side, was a pure transcendentalist without guile, accepting the transcendental ideas with no shadow of qualification; stating them with the concrete sharpness of scientific propositions, and applying them with the exactness of mathematical principles." [7] To speak of these philosophical traits as Parker's "religious side" is curious indeed, but it is linked with Frothingham's belief that Parker, while he was always a transcendentalist in sentiment, found it increasingly necessary to transfer transcendental principles to his own position to save it from insecure support on earlier non-transcendentalist grounds. He believed too that Parker was given the earnestness of his faith by transcendentalism and that this fact explained his "great power as a preacher." It was this faith, furthermore, which persuaded Parker that his was the gospel of the future, "the religion of enlightened men for the next thousand years." [8]

Another biographer, John White Chadwick, agrees with Frothingham in this regard, and finds also that "transcendentalism furnished him with an admirable formula of his personal religion." [9] As supporting evidence for his belief, Chadwick quotes the following statement from Parker's Journal:

[7] *Ibid.*, p. 307.
[8] Theodore Parker, *Theism, Atheism, and the Popular Theology*. (Vol. II of *The Works of Theodore Parker*), Preface.
[9] John White Chadwick, *Theodore Parker, Preacher and Reformer* (Boston, 1900), p. 178.

Then transcendentalism uses the other mode, the *a posteriori*. . . . . [In its argument for God] it finds signs and proofs of him everywhere, and gains evidence of God's existence in the limits of sensational experience. . . . At the ends of my arms are two major prophets, ten minor prophets, each of them pointing the transcendental philosopher to the infinite God of which he has consciousness without the logical process of induction.[10]

It is evident that this is inadequate for Chadwick's own conclusions, because he points out that Parker "lapsed from 'the high *a priori* road' to the plodding footpath of scientific induction." [11] Chadwick characterizes him intellectually by "a capacious understanding . . . his passion for facts, his stomach for statistics." [12] Though both transcendentalism and Parker, therefore, criticized earlier forms of sensationalism and traditional empiricism, Parker, even on Chadwick's account, was more interested in science and less in intuition than were the transcendentalists.

Chadwick places primary stress on the "personal equation," the distinguishing features of a unique type of transcendentalism. While he finds Parker to have been "a transcendentalist after the strictest manner of the sect," [13] he emphasizes the differences which existed between Parker and at least the major figures in the German tradition. The transcendentalism of Parker had an individual quality, which Chadwick ascribed to the fact that "it grew out of his character." [14] He makes reference to Parker's indebtedness to Jacobi, who

taught that God, the Soul, and Free Will were intuitive beliefs of the mind and had the same validity as Time, Space, and the External World as postulated by the demands of sensuous perception. Here certainly was a very close resemblance to Parker's

[10] *Ibid.*   [11] *Ibid.,* p. 177.   [12] *Ibid.*   [13] *Ibid.,* p. 110.
[14] *Ibid.,* p. 179.

transcendental consciousness of God, Immortality, and the Moral Law, but the resemblance was probably much more a matter of coincidence than a matter of sequence.[15]

Chadwick stresses the fact that "Jacobi's tone was unique among the German transcendentalists," [16] and finds Parker widely separated from others in the German tradition. He notes Parker's inability to accept Kant's "Moral Law given in consciousness, while God and Immortality are posited as intellectual forms, convenient for its operation, and for the ultimate reward of right doing." [17] Parker appeared to be still farther removed from Fichte's "towering idealism." Schelling's "monism" was also rejected, because, according to Chadwick, Parker had "a craving for simplicity." Furthermore, since Parker could use philosophy only as a handmaid for religion, he found, says Chadwick, little or no use for Hegel with "a Becoming for his God."

The question which this raises is whether Chadwick is not after all placing Parker on the fringe of German transcendentalism, when he stresses the peculiarities of Parker's thought and his criticism of the chief German exponents of transcendentalism. Is it not possible that though Parker received his major inspiration from German scholarship, he was more influenced by critical history than by the critical philosophy? The answer to this question may throw light on Parker's relation to New England as well as to German transcendentalism.

That Parker's immediate sources were French and English, rather than German, is hinted at by Chadwick when he asserts, in passing, that "there were more points of contact between Parker's philosophy and that of the French Eclectics, Cousin, Constant, and Jouffroy, and the English

[15] *Ibid.*, p. 175.   [16] *Ibid.*   [17] *Ibid.*, p. 176.

Germanists, Carlyle and Coleridge, than between it and any
German system except Jacobi's." [18] This demands investigation, for Chadwick failed to give adequate evidence. He
is more interested in Parker's position among "his American contemporaries." While he places Parker firmly in the
transcendentalist tradition in New England, Chadwick
points out that Parker's and Emerson's thoughts "were
cast in very different moulds." Emerson's thought he represents as cast in no mold at all, but as "a stream of tendency," his intuitions more feeble than Parker's sturdy
affirmations. The latter, according to Chadwick, lacked
metaphysical genius, and this trait separated him from
Emerson, Alcott, Ripley, Hedge, and Brownson; his was
an "English mind" and as such his genius was not metaphysical. Such a remark, even if it is not discriminating,
raises doubts concerning the intellectual relations between
Parker and his fellow New Englanders.

In a volume of *Studies in New England Transcendentalism,*[19] Harold Clarke Goddard uses a convenient, all too
convenient, method of determining who the New England
transcendentalists were. He repeats the loose and "elastic"
meanings of transcendentalism, making incidental references to several more exact technical meanings in the philosophy of Kant; he then points to Emerson's thought in
the opening sentences of *The Transcendentalist.* Goddard
then adds a number of "popular definitions," which he con-
siders to be "colloquial, satirical perversion[s] of the
term." [20] After this elaborate preparation, he announces
that he will not limit himself by any definition, but that he
will consider "almost exclusively . . . those whom . . .

[18] *Ibid.*   [19] New York, 1908.
[20] *Studies in New England Transcendentalism,* p. 6.

common consent has selected as the leaders of this movement." [21] The leaders by "common consent" are Alcott, Emerson, Parker, and Margaret Fuller. Even though Thoreau came to have "greater significance than . . . any of the other transcendentalists except Emerson," Goddard omits him from consideration because "the transcendentalist movement was already beyond its formative stage" when Thoreau came upon the scene.[22] Furthermore, William Ellery Channing, whose "temper and general spirit were singularly like those of the transcendentalists," and who was really "the first of the transcendentalists," [23] is nevertheless also excluded as a leader of the movement and is considered only because of his sympathetic and liberal attitudes toward its development.

Goddard discovers the sources of Parker's transcendentalism in his early life and in his reading. The first is an experience in Parker's youth, cited by Weiss, when he suddenly and clearly recognized the voice of his conscience dictating the difference between right and wrong; but surely the discovery of conscience was an eighteenth century commonplace, and no indication of transcendentalism. Following Frothingham's dubious suggestion, Goddard asserts that Parker inherited "his liking for the metaphysical" from his father and "a profoundly religious nature" from his mother. The second source, which appears most important to Goddard, is the impressive list of scholars whose works Parker read, foremost among these being Cousin, Jacobi, Kant, Fichte, Coleridge, and Spinoza. Were these in fact the foremost among the authors whom Parker studied? Goddard leaves us, obviously, without a critical answer to our central question.

21 *Ibid.,* pp. 8–9.   22 *Ibid.,* p. 9 note.   23 *Ibid.,* p. 28.

Clarence L. F. Gohdes, in his work devoted to *The Periodicals of American Transcendentalism*, was also confronted by the difficulty of determining what transcendentalism was, but proceeds, like Goddard, to state who the transcendentalists were. Stating that there were two types, Gohdes includes only "the narrow type," which included at least the following: William Ellery Channing, Emerson, Alcott, Brownson, Parker, Ripley, Francis, W. H. Channing, Hedge, Clarke, Furness, Dwight, Cranch, Peabody, and, possibly, Margaret Fuller. He explains that transcendentalism may have originated as "a natural reaction against the empirical philosophy of Locke"; [24] that its fundamental principle was "a belief in the infallibility of intuition"; [25] and that its terminology came from "foreign romantic doctrines," which had come to America principally through the reading of Coleridge and Cousin. It is Gohdes's belief that after Emerson withdrew from the scenes of controversy, Parker assumed the mantle, became "the chief transcendentalist," and, as the leader, enunciated the principles for the entire group.

While Gohdes attributes the designation "transcendentalist" generously to many figures in a broad and vague manner, he is confronted by the apparent differences between many of the individuals whom he so casually groups together. This is obvious when he says, "in attempting a study of the transcendental movement through the analysis of a manifestation of cooperative activity among its exponents, the student is perplexed by a pronounced element of individualism." [26] Gohdes continues, however, to

24 Clarence L. F. Gohdes, *The Periodicals of American Transcendentalism* (New York, 1931), p. 10.
25 *Ibid.*, pp. 10–11.   26 *Ibid.*, p. 12.

believe in the unity of the movement, explaining away individual differences among its leaders as "various phases of
the movement."

His account of the beginnings of *The Massachusetts
Quarterly Review* [27] is a good illustration of the ambiguous
position held by Parker. The group who conceived the plans
for this new periodical in 1847, only three years after
Emerson had given up *The Dial*,[28] consisted of Parker and
Emerson, Channing, Charles Sumner, Alcott, Thoreau,
Elliot Cabot, Dwight, Stone, Weiss, James Freeman Clarke,
Samuel G. Howe, and George Bradford. Parker finally
accepted the position as editor, but only after he had been
assured of the assistance of Emerson and Cabot. Parker
felt deeply the need for this new periodical; he was, consequently, ready to give it enthusiastic leadership. His
letter to Charles Sumner during the period when the position of editor was not yet filled indicated his interest.

I think we want a new journal, devoted to letters, poetry, art,
philosophy, theology, politics (in the best sense of that word),
and humanity in general. You know better than I the *North
American Review*, the *Christian Examiner*, etc. They are not
jusqu' au niveau de l'humanité. They will not be, cannot be. The
better minds of the age cannot express their thoughts therein. If
there were such a journal, ably conducted, it would have two
good influences: 1. It would strike a salutary terror into all the
Ultramontanists, and make them see that they did not live in the
Middle Ages—that they are not to be let alone dreaming of
the garden of Eden, but are to buckle up and work; 2. It would

[27] Additional material regarding history and content is given by Gohdes, *op. cit.*, pp. 157–193.
[28] *The Dial* was founded in 1840 and ended in 1844. Its founders and
contributors were, for the most part, members of the so-called "Hedge
Club," which had started in 1836. Accounts of the history and content
of this periodical are given in Gohdes, *op. cit.* (pp. 28–37), and G. W.
Cooke, "Introduction" for the Rowfant Club reprint of *The Dial* (1902).

spread abroad the ideas which now wait to be organized, some in
letters, some in art, some in institutions and practical life. . . .
Don't suppose I want to be one of the head and front of this
movement; I want no such thing, but not to appear at all. I wrote
to R. W. E. to ask him to take charge of such a work. If he fails,
what say you to that?[29]

Parker, as editor, concluded the "Farewell" at the end of
the third volume by confessing that "the periodical never
became what it was intended to be." [30] Emerson had failed
to support *The Review* enthusiastically; other transcendentalists, too, soon became lukewarm toward it. Why?
Because its editor was headed in a direction quite different
from their own? The career of the *Quarterly* may, therefore, throw light on our central problem.

The most recent comprehensive biography of Parker,
written by Henry Steele Commager,[31] also undertakes no
conclusive and critical answer to our central question.
Throughout this work, it is assumed that because of his
association with the members of the Hedge Club,[32] and his
general social activities, Parker belongs among the leaders
of New England transcendentalism.[33] But this does not

[29] Quoted from Weiss, *The Life and Correspondence of Theodore
Parker*, I, 267.
[30] Quoted by Gohdes, *op. cit.*, p. 166.
[31] Henry Steele Commager, *Theodore Parker, Yankee Crusader* (Boston, 1936); see also his two previous articles in the *New England Quarterly*, Vol. VI (Portland, 1933), and *The American Scholar*, Vol. III
(Summer, 1934).
[32] The "Hedge Club" was frequently called the "Transcendentalist
Club." Frederic Henry Hedge, in his essay on "The Transcendentalists," described its early nature and interests. Lists of its "members"
were given by Hedge, and he attempted to trace the origin of its name.
The Dial was described as "the product of the movement, and in some
sort its organ." For the full account, see James Elliot Cabot, *A Memoir
of Ralph Waldo Emerson* (Boston and New York, 1887), I, 244–246.
[33] Parker's scholarship is described as a "burrowing down to the very
subsoil of transcendentalism." See Commager, *Theodore Parker,
Yankee Crusader*, p. 63.

solve the more technical philosophical problem. Commager's distinctions are not very technical; he speaks of the transcendentalists both as "realists" ("never was there a more realistic, a more practical group of men than these high-flying souls of Concord and Boston" [34]) and as "idealists" ("they were all transcendentalists . . . they were all idealists." [35]); he finds their unity in their common belief in "the perfectibility of man and in the doctrine of progress." [36] Such vague social idealism fails to distinguish clearly the characteristic doctrines of the transcendentalists from the more general faith of the Enlightenment. Professor Commager does, however, indicate the need for caution when he suggests that, though Parker welcomed transcendentalism, crossed its threshold, and became absorbed in it, he

lived in the wonderful afterglow of the Enlightenment, reason tinged with humanitarianism, realism with romanticism. He lived in an age of faith and of hope, in a country where all things seemed possible. He was the heir of the rationalists, but their skepticism was irrelevant, here, in America. He was the heir of the idealists, and their abstractions seemed concrete, here in this brave new world. He was warmed by the first generous winds of science, and they brought certainty, not doubt. He knew that reason would triumph over unreason, that the righteous would be filled. He knew that Paradise Lost would be regained.[37]

Perhaps a fresh study of Parker's most characteristic interests, his favorite methods and his own most careful analyses may yield a more conclusive answer to our initial question than has previously been given. Specifically we must ask: How far did Parker express transcendentalism's more romantic aspects, such as those expressed by Schel-

[34] *Ibid.*, p. 58.   [35] *Ibid.*, p. 153.   [36] *Ibid.*   [37] *Ibid.*, pp. 195–196.

ling, Schleiermacher, and Emerson, and how far did he retain the more critical spirit of the Enlightenment and of
the Kantian methodology? It was clear to those who knew
him, and it must be equally obvious to all who read his
works, that he is a transitional figure, prophetic, yet cautious; he enjoyed the freedom that transcendentalism
offered, but he was uncomfortable in the midst of all its
enthusiasm, for he labored constantly to exhibit a respect
for scholarly and critical inquiry.

The questions to which this work is addressed are, therefore, best summarized in the following manner: To what
extent did Parker embrace New England transcendentalism? Did he hold to its romantic aspects or did he retain
the more critical spirit of the Enlightenment? Is he best
understood as the "prophetic preacher" of the new en-
thusiasms of transcendentalism, or as "one who kept the
faith of the Enlightenment and preached it with power"? [38]
Was he, "for all his justification of transcendentalism, . . .
closer to Franklin than to Emerson" [39] as Commager suggests? These questions are not merely academic in character; they are not raised in the interest of attaching an
oversimplifying label to Parker's thought. The intent is,
rather, to formulate the philosophical center around which
his critical theology revolves.

New England transcendentalism is difficult to define in
exact terms. It was hardly a movement; it never became a
philosophical system. It was, instead, a "faith," [40] an "en-

38 Herbert W. Schneider, *A History of Philosophy in America* (New
York, 1946), p. 262.
39 Henry Steele Commager, "Theodore Parker, Intellectual Gourmand,"
The American Scholar, III, 265.
40 Vernon Louis Parrington, *The Romantic Revolution in America*
(Vol. II of *Main Currents in American Thought,* New York, 1939), p.
381.

thusiasm," or a "ferment." Its central figures were seldom completely agreed; at the heights of its most ecstatic moments, it continued to be individualistic. At its foundation were two related but diverging "directives"—the one, a "full flowering of the 'New England Renaissance,' " [41] and the other, a reaction against its rationalism and a cultivation of sentiment and intuition. Historically, transcendentalism grew out of the Enlightenment. "Faith in the creative power of reason and the principles of secular moralism were taken over from the Enlightenment and embodied into transcendentalism without shock or reaction; romantic idealism was able to 'build its universe' on the foundations, rather than on the ruins, of the romantic faith in reason." [42] This aspect of transcendentalism which was based on "the critical philosophy," as Kant's system of the *Critiques* was called, glorified human reason because it was able by its own powers and methods to discover its own limitations. Kantian philosophy, and New England transcendentalism as well blended with this critical spirit a more romantic, idealistic strain. Whenever the movement is loosely described, this sentimental romanticism is usually allowed to represent the whole of transcendentalism.[43] The transcendental *critique* of Kant was, in fact, subordinated by most of his followers in Germany, England, and New England to the exploitation of his conception of the transcendental ego. Commager and Wellek [44] agree that "they [the New

[41] *Ibid.*, p. 379.
[42] Herbert W. Schneider, *A History of Philosophy in America*, p. 261.
[43] Emerson is commonly taken as the adequate expression of all New England transcendentalism.
[44] See Henry Steele Commager, *Theodore Parker, Yankee Crusader*, p. 153, and René Wellek, "The Minor Transcendentalists and German Philosophy," *The New England Quarterly*, XV (1942), 652–680. Schneider has pointed out, accurately, that only Hedge among the tran-

England transcendentalists] knew not Kant" and that the American Kant was "a misinterpreted Kant." Charles Theodore Christian Follen,[45] when he was appointed the first professor of German literature at Harvard in 1825, supplemented the information gained by various American students of German writings; but he knew little philosophy though he came from the center of idealism in Germany, and reinterpreted the Kantian categories as "innate ideas." [46] German writers other than Kant, but related in their philosophies, were in many respects more influential. For example, there was Friedrich H. Jacobi, who maintained that since the knowledge that can be gained through scientific demonstration alone is limited, man cannot hope to grasp "higher truth" without an act of immediate perception—that is, the intuitive knowledge of feeling. Similarly Friedrich Schleiermacher revolutionized the philosophy of religion with his theory of the *sense* of absolute dependence on God. The writings of Goethe, Schelling, Fichte, various of the German mystics, and the advocates of a *Glaubensphilosophie*, Herder and Hamaan, who based man's acquisition of fundamental truths on immediate apprehension and supported faith against the pantheism of Spinoza and the phenomenalism of the critical Kantians,

---

scendentalists, because he had studied and translated German romantic literature firsthand, knew the idealist philosophy from Kant to Hegel intimately; see his *A History of Philosophy in America*, pp. 277–278.
[45] For a full description of his career and interests see *The Works of Charles Follen with a Memoir of His Life* (5 vols., Boston, 1842).
[46] This is Wellek's statement: "The description of the *Critique of Pure Reason* is elementary and vitiated by Follen's repeated reference to time, space, and the categories as 'innate ideas'; he suspects Kant's system of leading to subjective idealism and skepticism; but then gives an exposition of the moral philosophy which shows far better insight and even critical acumen" (*The New England Quarterly*, XV, 1942, 658–659).

were much better known than the works of Kant himself.

The French Eclecticism of Cousin, Constant, and Jouffroy made its first thorough convert in a professor of philosophy at New York University, Caleb Sprague Henry,[47]
but it grew rapidly in popular favor among the New England transcendentalists. Transcendentalism's stress on
utopianism was almost wholly a French, St. Simonian heri-
tage. In their theory of knowledge, the Eclectics used the
concept of reason to denote any intuitive apprenhension of
unchangeable truths of moral life and of mathematics, and
claimed that such "unfinished truths" could not have come
through experience. Cousin's idealism, though it was introduced to America because it was believed to have been freed
from its "common sense" associations and to resemble more
fully the German romanticists,[48] in fact reflected much that
was central to the Scottish intuitive philosophy, especially
the attempt by its "founder," Thomas Reid of Glasgow, to
defend a *via media* between Hume and Berkeley, in asserting
that the mind obtains knowledge directly according to certain self-evident principles.

This Scottish philosophy, especially as it was systematized by Dugald Stewart, paved the way among the New
England Unitarians for transcendentalism. Most important of all the idealist sources was Coleridge, who popularized Schelling's idealism. James Marsh, professor of classics at the University of Vermont, adapted Coleridge's *Aids
to Reflection* [49] to American religious and philosophical

[47] See his edition of Victor Cousin's *Elements of Psychology* (New
York, 1834). It includes Henry's introduction, which set forth the
transcendentalist argument for absolute knowledge.
[48] For a fuller statement, see Schneider, *A History of American Philosophy,* p. 272.
[49] Kenneth Walter Cameron comments that this edition of Coleridge
was actually "a trumpet blast against the metaphysics of John Locke

needs. Inspiration or "revelation" was conceived to be the purest "reason," in matters touching life itself, whereas discursive or demonstrative "understanding" was reason in bondage to the world of sense phenomena. Coleridge was proclaimed as presenting "a philosophy that is religious, and a religion that is philosophical"; [50] philosophical, imaginative, reflection thus became a new type of religion, qualitatively different from both "revealed" and "natural" religion. "Reason," not identical with any other faculty, and more "spiritual" than science's analytical kind of truth, was given the position of revelation.[51] The a priori aspect of knowledge was thus glorified and made peculiarly religious. Coleridge's fellow romanticist, Thomas Carlyle, expounded a version of "natural supernaturalism" even more acceptable to the New England Scottish liberals. His best-known work, *Sartor Resartus*,[52] was somewhat reluctantly introduced by New England's leading figure, Ralph Waldo Emerson. Coleridge had already become Emerson's preeminent teacher; [53] but he recommended the book to Carlyle's American readers because of

as well as a commentary on contemporary thought in the United States" (*Emerson the Essayist*, Raleigh, N.C., 1945, I, 125 note.)

[50] The *Advertisement* for the Marsh Edition of *Aids to Reflection* (Burlington, Vt., 1829). This idea is developed in Ronald V. Wells, *Three Christian Transcendentalists* (New York, 1943).

[51] The relation between reason and experience was stated by Marsh (p. 45): "By experience only, I know that I have eyes; but then my reason convinces me that I must have had eyes in order to experience."

[52] The Emerson edition appeared in 1836.

[53] Other major sources were also evident. Henry David Gray has traced the development of the contrasting Platonism (derived from Channing and Coleridge) and subjectivism (from the German romanticists) in his volume entitled, *Emerson: a Statement of New England Transcendentalism as Expressed in the Philosophy of Its Chief Exponent* (Palo Alto, California, 1917). Cameron has given critical treatment to a variety of the philosophical traditions Emerson turned to for aid; see *Emerson the Essayist*, Vol. I.)

the manifest design of the work, which is, a Criticism upon the Spirit of the Age,—we had almost said, of the hour, in which we live; exhibiting, in the most just and novel light, the present aspects of Religion, Politics, Literature, Arts, and Social Life. Under all his gaiety, the writer has an earnest meaning, and discovers an insight into the manifold wants and tendencies of human nature, which is very rare among our popular authors. The philanthropy and the purity of moral sentiment, which inspire the work, will find their way to the heart of every true lover of virtue.[54]

Though neither Carlyle, nor Coleridge, nor the Germans, French or Scots expressed the peculiar character of New England transcendentalism, these "sources" are indicative of its dominant traits. Transcendentalism emphasized man's "spiritual" mastery over nature; it had more faith in its vision of the "harmony" of reason and natural law than in the scientific laboratory's "observational" discoveries of natural laws. "Communion" with nature took the place of a knowledge of nature. The transcendentalists wanted to "transcend" nature, its limitations and laws, so that the sovereignty of the spirit might be expressed. Without falling into orthodox supernaturalism, they desired to move above the confining limits of "natural" religion. They were dissatisfied with deistic doctrines and therefore emphasized various forms of mysticism. Their inspiration was monistic, but the union between God, man, and nature, was a monism of the spirit. They consequently rejected both the dualism of the Enlightenment and a growing materialistic monism. They expressed general disillusionment regarding "the age of reason," and turned to more subjective forms of utopianism. They repudiated any system which subordinated reason to experience, the individual will to in-

---

[54] Emerson, "Introduction" to *Sartor Resartus*.

stitutions, and the outer world to the inner. Emerson spoke for many of his fellow-transcendentalists when he said,

Let us inquire, to what end is nature? All science has one aim, namely, to find a theory of nature.

Nature always wears the colors of the spirit.

To the senses and the unrenewed understanding, belongs a sort of instinctive belief in the absolute existence of nature. In their view man and nature are indissolubly joined. Things are ultimates, and they never look beyond their sphere. The presence of reason mars this faith. . . . If the reason be stimulated to more earnest vision, outlines and surfaces become transparent, and are no longer seen; causes and spirits are seen through them. The best moments of life are these delicious awakenings of the higher powers, and the reverential withdrawing of nature before its God.

Of that ineffable essence which we call spirit, he that thinks most, will say least. We can foresee God in the coarse, and, as it were, distant phenomena of matter; but when we try to define and describe himself, both language and thought desert us, and we are as helpless as fools and savages. That essence refuses to be recorded in propositions, but when man has worshipped him intellectually, the noblest ministry of nature is to stand as the apparition of God. It is the organ through which the universal spirit speaks to the individual, and strives to lead back the individual to it.

Nature is so pervaded with human life that there is something of humanity in all and in every particular.

The world proceeds from the same spirit as the body of man. It is a remoter and inferior incarnation of God, a projection of God in the unconscious.[55]

Such thinking was intended to cultivate the poetic imagination. It emphasized the individual soul's capacity in in-

---

[55] *Nature, Addresses, and Lectures, Emerson's Complete Works*, vol. I, (Boston, 1887), 10, 17, 54–55, 65–66, 67, and 68.

tuition and contemplation, reliance upon the individual self, and a general reaction against so-called spiritual institutions and organizations. "Reason" was reinterpreted as a personal possession, divorced from cooperative understanding, and having the power to perceive truth privately. That a corporate life of the spirit was foreign to the revolutionary self-reliance of the transcendentalists can be seen, for example, in their either leaving the church and its corporate worship or interpreting its fellowship individualistically.

In its opposition to common sense and vulgarity, both in religion and art, transcendentalism took pride in its literary culture. This pride was made explicit in its contempt for secondhand discoveries of truth. It caused them to despise intellectual institutions as well as tradition and conservatism. It led to the exaggerated ambitions of the transcendentalists to be emancipated, cosmopolitan, and poetic in their attitudes and speech. While they admitted little faith in book knowledge, their hope of being genuine authors, original contributors to human wisdom, led them in their writing and lecturing to an oracular style. These are the dominant traits by which a New England transcendentalist can be recognized and which serve commonly to define the type. Of these traits Emerson has been regarded as the chief incarnation.

How far did Parker exhibit these traits? Which of its tenets and sources were his? To what other interests did he devote himself? What was his relationship to those who embraced and expounded this faith most fully, particularly Emerson? These are among the questions to which this work is addressed.

A somewhat cursory examination of most secondary sources suggests immediately that Parker and Emerson traditionally belong together; their frequent companionship, their cooperative journalistic efforts, and some of their characteristic terms and ideas support their relationship as colleagues. Parker was often inclined to praise Emerson as a "man of literary genius . . . who never appeals to a mean motive, who uplifts and inspires"; [56] "the most American, [and] almost the most cosmopolitan of our writers"; [57] the "awakener" of spiritual, manly or natural religion "in the great Saxon heart of the Americans and Britons"; [58] the "revoker" of "all institutions but the law of his own nature"; and the lover of nature, who has "the synthetic vision of the poet." [59] After Parker's death, Emerson's regard for his friend found expression in an address given at a memorial service in Music Hall, June 15, 1860, [60] and in a later essay entitled "Historic Notes of Life and Letters in New England," in which Parker is described as

an excellent scholar, in frank and affectionate communication with the best minds of his day, yet the tribune of the people, and the stout reformer to urge and defend every cause of humanity with and for the humblest of mankind. . . . He stood altogether for practical truth, and so to the last. He used every day and hour of his short life, and his character appeared in the last

[56] *Lessons from the World of Matter and the World of Man,* a selection of "familiar lessons" from some of Parker's sermons between 1849 and 1859; this is Vol. V in *The Collected Works of Theodore Parker;* the quotation referred to is from p. 86.

[57] "The Writings of Ralph Waldo Emerson," the *Massachusetts Quarterly Review* (March, 1850); this article is reprinted in *The Collected Works of Theodore Parker,* VIII, 63.

[58] "The Revival of Religion Which We Need," a sermon delivered on Sunday, April 11, 1858; it was printed in pamphlet form, and appears in *The Collected Works of Theodore Parker,* IV, 422.

[59] "The Writings of Ralph Waldo Emerson," pp. 66 and 70.

[60] This address appears in the centenary edition of Emerson's works, and in O. B. Frothingham's *Theodore Parker, a Biography,* pp. 549–557.

moments with the same firm control as in the midday of strength. I habitually apply to him the words of a French philosopher who speaks of "the man of nature who abominates the steam engine and the factory. His vast lungs breathe independence with the air of the mountains and the woods." [61]

Despite his frequent praise, Parker was also devastatingly critical of Emerson, particularly of his later writings, and at the precise points which separate them; these criticisms therefore, shed light on Parker's fundamental interests. He complained that "Emerson's works do not betray any exact scholarship"; that they show no "indications of exact mental discipline"; that his is "not the analytic eye of the naturalist"; that "he undervalues the logical, demonstrative, and historical understanding"; that because he "also undervalues the affections, . . . his man, who is the measure of all things, is not the complete man"; that he "proceeds by the way of intuition, sensational or spiritual," revoking both the inductive and deductive methods; and that he "is sometimes extravagant in the claims made for his own method, and maintains that ecstasy [62] is the natural and exclusive mode of arriving at new truths, while it is only one mode." [63] This extensive criticism was matched on Emerson's part by his opinion that Parker was "no artist.

[61] This sketch is available in several editions; it appears in Emerson's *Lectures and Biographical Sketches*, Vol. X of the complete *Works* (Boston, 1887), pp. 324–325.

[62] Parker defined what he believed Emerson meant by "ecstasy" as "the state of intuition in which the man loses his individual self consciousness" ("The Writings of Ralph Waldo Emerson," p. 83). He criticized those who devoted themselves exclusively to this method; especially did he criticize Jacob Boehme and Emmanuel Swedenborg, "who most completely surrender themselves to this mode of action, and show how poor and insufficient it is. All that mankind has learned in this way is little compared with the results of reflection, of meditation, and careful, conscientious looking after truth" (*ibid.*, pp. 83–84).

[63] *Ibid.*, pp. 69, 70, 80, and 83.

Highly refined persons might easily miss in him the element of beauty. What he said was mere fact, almost offended you, so bald and detached; little cared he." [64] Parker repeatedly accused Emerson of having exaggerated his "idiosyncracy into a universal law" by believing that "books are only for one's idle hours" and his usual discouragement of "hard and continuous thought, conscious modes of argument or discipline."

The method of nature is not ecstasy, but patient attention. Human nature avenges herself for the slight he puts on her, by the irregular and rambling character of his own productions. The vice appears more glaring in the Emersonidae, who have all the agony without the inspiration, who affect the unconscious, write even more ridiculous nonsense than their "genius" requires; are sometimes so child-like as to become mere babies, and seem to forget that the unconscious state is oftener below the conscious than above it, and that there is an ecstasy of folly as well as of good sense.

He must regret that his extravagant estimate of ecstasy, intuitive unconsciousness, has been made and has led some youths and maids astray.[65]

Parker's criticisms of Emerson's exclusive dependence on the "intuitive unconsciousness," though genial, were nonetheless sincere and serious. While both Emerson and Parker rejected the so-called "design argument," their views of nature and human nature differed widely. Emerson discovered through introspection and intuition the divinity of the soul, not merely the religious faculty; he spiritualized nature with his doctrine of final causes and compensations, paying little heed to natural law in natural history. Parker

[64] Emerson, "Historic Notes of Life and Letters in New England," p. 324.
[65] "The Writings of Ralph Waldo Emerson," pp. 84 and 97.

did not accept this romanticizing of nature; he looked to the demonstrative faculties and to human history, rather than to spiritual harmonies, for the revelation of human nature. He did not idealize the soul as a "microcosm," but commended study of the developmental process of human nature; Parker's thought was therefore closer to evolutionism than to transcendentalism. He believed that Emerson, through his exaggeration of a single "mode" of receiving truth, had "no total balance of all the faculties"; he had not

love enough . . . to balance his intellect, his conscience, and his faith in God; . . . there appears a worship of the infinite God far transcending all we find in Taylor or Edwards, in Fénélon or Channing; it is reverence, it is trust, the worship of the conscience, of the intellect; it is obedience, the worship of the will; *it is not love,* the worship of the affections.[66]

In practice, therefore, Parker remained within the church and aimed at the internal reform of Christian institutions and theology, whereas Emerson established a "secular pulpit" and attempted to reform man and society apart from specifically Christian forms.[67] With the surrender of affection, Emerson's ethics took on what Parker called "a certain coldness; he is a man running alone, and would lead others to isolation, not society." [68] "The genius of Emerson soon moved from the clerical constellation, and stood

[66] *Ibid.,* p. 98–99.

[67] Emerson says this very concisely. In a letter to Parker conveying an invitation to visit a group at Cincinnati he says, "I infer that the practical difficulty in begging a visit from you is this. They wish to hear your sermons or theological lectures, and find it a little awkward to *buy* these. My lectures, being secular, are good purchaseable wares, advertiseable at fixed prices. My inviters took no risk, as the public came and paid. But I suppose they do not wish to ask the public to pay you for what they wish the public to hear." From a letter dated July 2, 1850; *The Letters of Ralph Waldo Emerson,* ed. by Ralph L. Rusk (6 vols., New York, 1939), IV, 218.

[68] "The Writings of Ralph Waldo Emerson," p. 98.

forth alone, a fixed and solitary star." [69] In this extreme "love of individuality," Emerson appeared to Parker as "unconsciously deprived . . . of the grace of order," [70] not only in his "love to particularize" but also in his failure to state his thoughts in an "orderly arrangement"; "Emerson builds a rambling Gothic church with an irregular outline, a chapel here, and a tower there, you do not see why." [71] "It is not doctrine he teaches—his own creed is not well defined." [72] These are differences which clearly emerge from the criticisms.

These differences are given further illustration in the journalistic adventures of the two men. When Margaret Fuller announced in the spring of 1842 that she could not continue to assume the editorship of *The Dial* and wrote to Emerson suggesting that he or Parker take it over, Emerson replied: "I had rather undertake it alone than with any partnership of oversight such as Mr. Parker or Mr. Ripley for example." [73] He followed this plan and said it was because he had "so little skill in partnership." [74] But other difficulties, specifically between Emerson and Parker, paralleled this individualism. When Parker later presented various materials for publication at the editor's request, Emerson was irritated by the articles and criticized Parker for wanting to transform the fundamental character of the journal. The article on John Pierpont [75] is a case in point.

[69] "Experience as a Minister," one of Parker's biographical writings, which he composed at Santa Cruz shortly before his death. It was sent to his Boston congregation, and it appears in *The Collected Works of Theodore Parker,* Vol. XIII; the citation is from p. 294.

[70] "The Writings of Ralph Waldo Emerson," p. 102.

[71] *Ibid.,* p. 104.

[72] "The Revival of Religion Which We Need," p. 422.

[73] *The Letters of Ralph Waldo Emerson,* III, 35.   [74] *Ibid.*

[75] Parker entitled it, "The Proceedings of an Ecclesiastical Council in the Case of the . . . Hollis Street Meeting House and the Rev. John Pierpont." Though Emerson had requested it for the spring edition,

Parker suggested that Emerson might wish to omit it if he
cared to and said, "I am not a *baby* to be vexed with you." [76]
Emerson replied that Parker had spent too much time and
effort on "that most unpoetic, unspiritual, and un-Dialled
John Pierpont," but that he had sent it unread to the
printer "purely out of honor to the contributor." [77] A review of Parker's *Discourse on Religion,* which Emerson
had promised would be prepared by William Channing but
which was never published,[78] is another illustration of an
undercurrent of difficulties. Furthermore, in one of his
letters to Emerson, Parker commented that some of the
articles contained "too much *Dialese.*" [79]

Various incidents connected with the *Massachusetts
Quarterly Review* throw still more specific light on the differences between Emerson and Parker. Parker's enthusiastic leadership as editor of the *Review* was disconcerting
to Emerson, though he, with Cabot, had pledged their support and editorial guidance. When its first issue appeared
at the close of 1847, Emerson, writing from England, made
the following observation: "their journal is of good spirit
and has much good of Agassiz,[80] but no intellectual tone,
such as is imperatively wanted; no literary skill even, and,
without a loftier note than any in this number, it will sink
in a North American at once." [81] When he returned to

---

and though Parker had complied with this request, the article did not
appear until October, 1842.

[76] Parker's letter to Emerson of July 8, 1842, which is quoted in the
Rusk edition, III, 70, note 270.

[77] Emerson's letter to Parker of September 8, 1842, *ibid.,* p. 86.

[78] A discussion of this difficulty is evident in Emerson's letter to Parker
of June 30, 1842; see *ibid.,* pp. 68–69, and note 266.

[79] Parker's letter to Emerson of July 8, 1842, *op. cit.,* p. 70.

[80] The reference is to "The Life and Writings of Agassiz," which
Gohdes (*op. cit.,* p. 166) says was an article written by Cabot.

[81] Emerson's letter to Lidian of January 8 and 12, 1848; *Letters,* IV, 4.

America the following autumn, Emerson immediately set out to bring an end to the *Review*. He believed that it served no good purpose, since its primary contributors could sell their material more readily independently than through its pages, and thus lesser contributors were being driven by the editor to write for him. Moreover, although it was launched to meet the apparent need for a good political journal, "we have found no new political writer." [82] And though he had not yet actually worked at the journal, Emerson felt it was a burden on his hands; he had other more important work to do: "Now I have nothing to spare, not an hour, not a page to waste, and cannot think of throwing away my good time, without some prospect of adequate benefit to accrue: we have too few scholars to justify any profligacy of spending." [83] This attitude, together with Parker's apparently unauthorized promise to the *Review's* subscribers that since "the senior editor . . . has now returned . . . [he] will of course contribute to its columns," [84] led Emerson to submit his resignation as one of the editors and as a regular contributor. An excerpt from his letter to William Emerson at this time reveals his chagrin:

I am myself harassed not a little by the pertinacity with which Mr. Theodore Parker insists on printing—against my express declaration to him—that RWE is an Editor of the Mass. Q. Review, and will write in it; and then throws himself for defense on the dysentery which is killing his family, and the general claims of Literature, etc., etc., Who can escape Cant? [85]

[82] Emerson's letter to Parker, August 17? 1848, *ibid.*, pp. 106–107.
[83] Emerson's letter of August 26, 1848, *ibid.*, p. 108.
[84] *The Massachusetts Quarterly Review*, September, 1848, pp. 527–528.
[85] Emerson's letter to William Emerson of September 4, 1848; the *Letters*, IV, 111.

Cabot also resigned at the same time. But, because Parker believed that closing the *Review* was unfair to both the public and the publishers—and, no doubt, also because he needed this "organ as much as a political chief would," [86] as Emerson put it—he offered to carry on alone. The publishers accepted his offer, and he later invited Emerson to contribute to the journal if he chose to.[87] Nevertheless, the bitterness remained. Emerson confided the difficulties as he saw them to his brother: Parker's energy and resoluteness were disturbing; Parker's belief that his unpopularity would prohibit his contributing to other journals appeared wholly imaginary to Emerson; and, "though he does not care for that which alone would interest me in a journal, the *spirit and interests* of my literary friends, yet he reckoned me as an available party." Emerson concluded that "we may both write very well for one journal; but I should not be interested in one that was mainly his." [88]

The basic difference between Emerson and Parker, according to this evidence, is that of divergent fundamental interests and tastes. Parker was headed in a direction quite different from Emerson. His repeated attempts at commanding in his literary work a critical interest was opposed to the poetic, spiritual, "Dialled" Emerson. When the *Review* was regretfully, and abruptly, concluded, the editor was aware that Emerson's failure to join him was in part responsible. Our hypothesis is supported by these observations: though Parker and Emerson have often been

---

86 *Ibid.*, p. 114.
87 Parker's letter to Emerson of September 9, 1848, which Rusk included, *ibid.*, p. 113, reveals this.
88 Emerson's letter to William Emerson of September 21, 1848; *ibid.*, pp. 113–114. (Italics mine.)

assigned positions of close affinity, particularly by Parker's biographers, their purposes and interests reveal wide divergences. The conclusion is quite clear: "all the biographies of Parker bear testimony to the close relations of Emerson and Parker, and their writings indicate how wide apart they were in much of their thinking." [89]

[89] George Willis Cooke, "Notes" regarding "The Writings of Ralph Waldo Emerson," *The Collected Works of Theodore Parker*, pp. 505–506.

Chapter 2

BIBLICAL CRITICISM AND
CRITICAL THEOLOGY

AMONG THE EARLIEST of Theodore Parker's scholarly interests was his study of Biblical writings from the viewpoint of historical and literary criticism. He was one of the first theologians in America to appreciate the far-reaching significance of this "scientific" methodology. He was convinced that from it would come a general advance in all the sciences, that it would give dignity to free inquiry in the most conservative areas of human learning, and that it would support both moral and ecclesiastical reform.

His first introduction to the methods and scope of Biblical criticism was a result of his editorial work for *The Scriptural Interpreter* [1] during his senior years at the Divinity School. In the course of his preparation of exegetical and historical articles, Parker became aware of the writings of such foremost German scholars of the Old and New Testaments as Johann Gottfried Eichhorn and Wilhelm M. L. De Wette. This early interest, together with the encouragement he was given by his lifelong friend, Dr. Convers Francis,[2] and by such colleagues as George Ripley

[1] This modest publication was founded in 1831 by Ezra Stiles Gannett for the purpose of family instruction. The complete file of this review is catalogued in the Boston Public Library.
[2] Dr. Francis was first a minister in Watertown, Mass.; he later was invited to be professor of Biblical Theology at Harvard.

and Frederic Hedge, soon led Parker to begin his first serious scholarly work. The basis for his work was De Wette's learned *Lehrbuch der historisch-kritischen Einleitung in die kanonischen und apocryphischen Bücher des Alten Testementes.*[3] This volume was among those responsible for Parker's praise of German scientific and theological works. He commented that Germany was "the only land where theology was . . . studied as a science, and developed with scientific freedom."[4] The six years he devoted to the intensive study of De Wette's work was of significant influence on Parker's characteristic methodological interests and his later theological views. It led directly to the collecting of his large and diversified private library.[5]

Parker was deeply interested in De Wette's *Introduction* for several reasons. He was attracted by its theological liberalism, an approach which De Wette found in Jacob Friedrich Fries who in turn followed Kant.[6] Theological liberalism was, in Parker's opinion, the only viewpoint compatible with a strictly scientific use of the tools of critical study. As a result, his repeated attacks on the conservative conclusions of such scholars as Havernik and Horne, and of his American contemporaries, Moses Stuart, Edward Rob-

[3] Parker's edition of this *Introduction* appeared in 1843. He had begun the work in the late summer of 1836.
[4] "Experience as a Minister," p. 315.
[5] Thomas Wentworth Higginson, in his article on Parker in the *Atlantic Monthly,* Vol. VI (October, 1860), commented that this collection of some 13,000 volumes was "the richest private library in Boston." Higginson's "Report to the Trustees of the Boston Public Library on the Parker Library" gives a detailed account of the nature of the library; this Report has been reprinted in the *Bibliography and Index to the Works of Theodore Parker* (Boston, 1910), pp. 1–10.
[6] Fries was professor of Philosophy at Heidelberg and Jena. His major book was entitled *Neue oder anthropologische Kritik der Vernunft* (Jena, 1807).

inson, and Andrews Norton, usually centered on their theological dogmatism and their failure to engage in "negative" criticism. He believed that their basic theological bias
limited their use of the critical method, but that De Wette's
liberalism permitted him to practice his criticism freely.
This work also supplied Parker with a complete survey of
previous Biblical scholarship. This storehouse of information stimulated Parker's extraordinary love of encyclo-
pedic learning.[7] Parrington called him "the greatest scholar
of his generation of New England ministers," attributing
much of his vast learning to his interest in German Biblical
scholarship; he had, said Parrington, "the latest results of
higher criticism on his study table, [and] he was critically
trained to separate historical fact from ecclesiastical tradition." [8] De Wette's volume also gave Parker ample op-
portunity to display his linguistic erudition. In his com-
pleted translation of the *Einleitung*, Parker included
translations as well as the originals of all Latin, Greek, and
Hebrew passages. Then, too, while De Wette's text had
been prepared as a guide for teachers and scholars already
engaged in Biblical study, Parker saw in his edition, with
its extensive elaborations of difficult and disputed passages,
its annotated bibliography and rearrangements in the outline, its translations of important source materials, and its
storehouse of illustrative material which had been added
from both the Church Fathers and modern critical sources,
a comprehensive encyclopedia of Biblical learning. He
wanted to make the result of his work an edifying and accu-

[7] That Parker's love of learning was extraordinary has been widely
commented upon by those who have written about him.
[8] Vernon Louis Parrington, *The Romantic Revolution in America*
(Vol. II of *Main Currents of American Thought*, New York, 1939),
p. 417.

rate source book which could be understood not only by the scholars, but by "the American public."

Parker's fundamental reason for using this work as the basis for his critical studies was that De Wette's aim was compatible with his own; the underlying plan of criticism he found especially attractive. Parker often stated alternate conclusions regarding intricate textual and historical problems, and sometimes set forth solutions contradictory to those offered by De Wette. But in regard to the essential aims of criticism, their opinions were identical.

Since the object of an introduction to the Bible is the history of the Bible, its scientific character is *historico-critical;* that is, the Bible is to be considered as an historical phenomenon, in a series with other such phenomena, and entirely subject to the laws of historical inquiry. The consideration of it in a religious view— that is, according to the dogma of inspiration and revelation— falls within the department of introduction only so far as this dogma is connected with the history of the origin of the Bible. This dogma itself, therefore, is likewise to be treated historically.[9]

Whereas Eichhorn had devoted his study primarily to textual problems, De Wette was among the earliest to use historical inquiry as the method central to Biblical scholarship. Parker agreed with this, and agreed also with De Wette's attempt to relate the historical and the exegetical aspects of criticism.

[Critical study] furnishes the historical materials which are necessary to the explanation of the Bible. To treat it, then, as a peculiar theological exercise has not only an external advantage in a literary and academic respect, but also an internal advantage for the science itself.[10]

[9] "Translator's Preface," *A Critical and Historical Introduction to the Canonical Scriptures of the Old Testament* (Boston, 1843), I, 3.
[10] *Ibid.,* p. 4.

Parker acknowledged his indebtedness to De Wette for conceiving of criticism in this comprehensive manner. While he stated that "the design of criticism is *to determine what was originally written by the author*," [11] which is the problem central to textual criticism, Parker followed De Wette in his belief that criticism generally leaves the scholar free "to pass judgment" on the text and at times to engage in "critical conjecture." Parker believed that this role of the critic should be used primarily in the interpretation of specific Biblical passages. Consequently, he often compared the conclusions of De Wette with those arrived at by Eichhorn, Michaelis, and Bertholdt; [12] in the end, he usually stated his own judgment as well. Parker, nevertheless, also believed that the critic should be prepared to state a view of the Bible as a whole. He believed that such a view should be "educated," that it should repeatedly distinguish between mythology and history, and that it should "take the Bible for what it is worth." [13]

In his study of the Old Testament, he gave attention first to the historical formation of the canon, making note of the earliest recorded acceptance of such writings as the law and the prophets and then surveying the later additions of the "writings" and the historical documents. Most of his study was concentrated on the acceptance of the Old Testament by the Church Fathers and the Christian community. This historical study of the canon was followed by his study of numerous literary problems, such as the authorship and

11 *Ibid.*
12 Johann D. Michaelis's *Einleitung* was widely read among Biblical critics; it was, nevertheless, not so prominent a work as Eichhorn's *Einleitung* . . . (3 vols., Leipsig, 1780–83), or the later enlargement of this work of 1795. Bertholdt's work was similar to De Wette's, since it attempted to combine the historical with the critical method.
13 *A Discourse of Matters Pertaining to Religion,* in *Works,* I, 333.

dates of various writings, and certain grammatical difficulties.[14] Textual criticism was his most useful tool. Parker
followed De Wette in the traditional division of the Hebrew
books, though he was acquainted with Bertholdt's characteristic treatment of the Old Testament as a unity. He
concluded that the alleged Mosaic authorship of the Pentateuch must be rejected, since these writings exhibited at
least two distinct and sometimes contradictory documents.
He traced the Elohistic document with the help of Stähelin [15] and assigned it to the period of Samuel or Saul—between 1120 and 1055 B.C. The Jehovistic document he
attributed to a date later than the Elohistic; [16] while he
compared the documents with care, he did not engage in extensive independent criticism. Parker interpreted Genesis as
an introduction to the Hexateuch and as the best Old Testament illustration of the blending of mythology and saga,
and of these and history. While he believed that both myth
and saga rise above "the ordinary laws of historical cau-
sality," a myth is "an idea clothed in facts" while a saga
"contains facts penetrated and transformed by ideas." [17]
He then differentiated the passages which recalled an ideal
antiquity from those which related the intervention of the
miraculous or supersensuous in history. He also distinguished between the sections which expressed "theocratical
pragmatism," which makes of God the immediate cause of

[14] Parker's source for the study of Hebrew grammar was the work
of the eminent scholar, then recognized as the most competent in his
field, Friedrich H. W. Gesenius, upon whose work much of De Wette's
critical study was also based.
[15] Stähelin's work was entitled *Studien und Kritichen* (1835).
[16] In the matter of assigning these documents to this early period,
Parker followed Bleek and Tuch, whose viewpoints were similar to
Rosenmüller and therefore near to, but less radical than, De Wette's.
[17] *A Critical and Historical Introduction*, II, 23.

all events, and "theocratical mythology," which interprets all divine influence in history as revelation. The remaining books of the Hexatauch, with the exception of Leviticus, were grouped together in Parker's analysis, since they were conceived of as a history of the establishment of the Hebrew theocracy. That this first division of the Old Testament constituted a rationalization of the legal foundations of Israel based upon the epics in Genesis and culminating in Leviticus was an interesting conclusion. He stated some of this in the following letter:

In reading the Pentateuch, did you ever notice marks of a distinct plan and design on the part of the compiler? It seems to me there is an almost rythmical progress of theocratic ideas from end to end of Genesis. 1. God makes the world in six days, so that *he may rest on the Sabbath.* 2. Abel's offering of slain-beasts, the first-born of his flock, and God's acceptance thereof, consecrates that kind of sacrifice, and perhaps favors the *pastoral* life, and places it above the *agricultural.* 3. Noah makes the Levitical distinction between *clean* and *unclean* animals; *blood* is forbidden to be used as food; a *covenant* is made with the race, and God is pleased and *rendered placable* by sacrifice; vengeance for *blood* is denounced, and agriculture perhaps discouraged (IX, 10). 4. A preparation being made, the theocracy soon begins, and Jehovah makes a *covenant* with Abraham and his race, who are to be *the peculiar people;* circumcision is established as the *distinctive sign* thereof. 5. The origin or destination of all the neighboring nations is proved. . . . 6. The *claim to Palestine* is made perfect (1) by the provisions and commands of God, (2) by the law of inheritance . . . , (3) by the family residing there, (4) having their ancestral tomb in it, solemnly ceded to them, for a valuable consideration, and the whole transacted in the most public manner. 7. God's blessing attended them even in Egypt. . . . 8. Then comes the consecration of the first-born of man and beast. The Passover, the *feast of tabernacles,* the consecration of the Levites, etc., the temple tax a half-a-shekel, and the whole Levitical law with all its fringes, and ridiculous tabernacle cherubim and the like. It seems to me that all this is very artificial and notes the successive steps in this great national form. I don't accuse the compilers, since I presume they meant only to make an epic, not to write a history, though we very foolishly refuse to take it for what it is, but would make it suit our ridiculous fancy and then —thrust the authorship on the Deity.[18]

Parker also explained the uniformity of the historical writings by asserting that "the theocratical men," whose interests included history and law, were prophets and priests who worked cooperatively in "historical societies" or in "academies of science," the prophets transcribing the annals of court historians while the priests compiled the legal codes. Parker thus departed from De Wette's predominantly historical emphasis as he distinguished between the historical narratives and the book of Leviticus. He concluded that this document, while priestly in character, does not belong with the other Elohistic writings, although it may have been edited by the Elohist; only the technical phraseology of the introductory and concluding formulae coincide with the Elohist document. Following De Wette's conclusion with regard to Deuteronomy, Parker agreed that, because it reflected Josiah's reform measures, it clearly belonged to the later period of Hebrew history when the worship of God on "the high places" was already forbidden. This placed the book in about the year 621 B.C., and this conclusion, based on De Wette's study, solved one of the foremost critical problems in Parker's day. Parker also followed De Wette with regard to the book of Joshua. The central figure in this work was "the hero of all

18 Letter to Convers Francis, February 29, 1840, in a collection owned by the Boston Public Library.

the theocratic conquests and acquisitions" [19] of the Hebrew nation, as Moses was the sole hero of its legislation; the narrative centering around Joshua was interpreted as another chapter in the history of Israel. The numerous contradictions in the document were noted, and special attention was given to its inaccuracies and "errors." Parker then assigned it, because of its references to the "Book of the Law" and its Levitical spirit, to a late exilic date. In so doing he deviated from De Wette and followed such critics as Hase, Masius, and Maurer.

Parker made several other notable statements regarding the "historical" writings. He concluded that the book of the Judges was compiled by an historian in northern Palestine at a late date, and that the compiler allegedly related the actual history of a given period of Israel's theocratic development, but selected only the incidents which showed "that suffering follows sin, and obedience to the law of Jehovah always secures tranquillity and national happiness." [20] Parker called such a "scheme" of historical narration unscientific and therefore objectionable. He cited instances in the books of Samuel in which prophecies were obviously inserted into the text after the related events had taken place, thereby transforming prophecy into judgment. Moreover, history is subordinated in importance to biography, chronological outline is more legendary than historical, and, finally, because the two books of Samuel reveal no predominantly sacerdotal interest, they belong to an early period.

The books of the Kings were interpreted as relating the history of Israel from the time of David's death to the be-

---

[19] *A Critical and Historical Introduction*, p. 171.
[20] *Ibid.*, p. 195.

ginning of the Exile; they illustrate a retrogression in historical narration when compared with the other literature of the monarchial period. Parker concluded that the stories of Elijah and Elisha belong to an early oral tradition, and that the two separate documents were finally woven together into a single legend. He assumed, with Eichhorn and Bertholdt as opposed to De Wette, that the historical data in these narratives and the two books as a whole came either from private historical records or from royal annals. His conjecture that compilation did not take place until the Exilic period was based on

the whole spirit of the book; with the constant reference to the Mosaic Law; the aversion to sacrifices on the high places; the stiff prophetic pragmatism; the gloomy view of the history; the legends and exaggerations; [and certain] peculiarities of language.[21]

Parker believed that the books of the Chronicles were written by priests. He rejected the interpretation given in the Talmudic tractate Baba Bathra, and cited by others with authority, that these books were written by Ezra, and he also rejected Bertholdt's view that they were accurate historical documents. Parker was convinced that they were designed by priestly writers as an indictment of the history of the Davidic kingdom, with its domestic tribal antagonisms and the final triumph of Judah. The Chronicles, he said, attempted to prove that Judah had become superior because it observed the law, engaged in Levitical worship, and was led by pious kings.

Parker also departed from De Wette in his treatment of the "semi-historical" book of Ruth. He did not follow the extreme view set forth by Bertholdt that the entire work is

21 *Ibid.*, p. 248.

fictional, believing, rather, that the narrative was first circulated orally and later enriched in literary significance by the added genealogy of David. He assigned it to a late period in Hebrew history, since its compilation evidently followed the Deuteronomic prohibition of the marriage of Hebrews with foreign women.[22] He grouped together the books of Ezra and Nehemiah because both deal with the period of restoration following the Exile, and suggested that since they are historically continuous with the Chronicles, they may be ascribed to the same compiler. He accepted De Wette's conclusions regarding the periods covered by these works: Ezra from the beginning of the restoration period (that is, from 536 B.C.) down to the seventh year of Artaxerxes Longimanus (458 B.C.); Nehemiah, continuing the narration, from 444 to 404 B.C. The book of Esther was interpreted as a "patriotic romance" primarily fictional in character. Parker's conclusion that it was compiled after the destruction of the Persian monarchy was supported by an unusually extensive study of characteristically late literary forms; he cited numerous illustrations of the interpolation of Persian words into the Hebrew text. This conclusion, with the others regarding "the so-called books of history," illustrates Parker's tendency to exercise private judgment and his interest in some of the most technical aspects of Biblical criticism.

The discussion of the prophetic writings began with the distinction between prophets as *seers* and as *interpreters of God;* Samuel, Elijah, and Elisha were referred to as *seers*, while the "major" prophets, Amos, Hosea, Isaiah, Ezekiel, and Jeremiah, were believed to "speak for" God. This dis-

[22] See Deuteronomy, Chapter 23; this prohibition is repeated in Ezra 9:1ff., and Nehemiah 13:1-3, 23-27.

tinction had been well clarified by De Wette. Parker followed it, and then quoted Eichhorn on the vocation of a great prophet to serve as a counselor to his king and his countrymen in periods of emergency; his role should not be limited to either exciting or satisfying the peoples' curiosity as a foreteller. This tendency to minimize the place of prophetic predictions has important implications. It meant that these predictions should be studied as "expressions of anxiety"; they should be viewed in the historical context of what occasioned them, rather than ascribing them validity only when they are historically fulfilled. It matters little, therefore, whether or not they have historical consequences; some were apparently added to the text after the event had occurred; others, such as Jeremiah's prediction of seventy years in Exile, Ezekiel's oracle against Tyre, and many of the Messianic prophecies, were never fulfilled. In either case, the prophecy is still important, because of what gave rise to it. The prophet reflected a national crisis.

Parker also believed that prophets, as opposed to priests, serve the cause of truth courageously because they labor continuously toward the purification and extension of both religion and morality. His interest in the Hebrew prophets centered, consequently, in their importance as historical figures who sensed cultural and religious emergencies and whose pronouncements expressed Israel's historical crises. He concluded that the major prophets' utterances were always spontaneous, and that both the signs and symbolic acts which accompanied the prophecies were equally unpremeditated. From the literary point of view, Parker found that the style is usually poetic and often symmetrically lyrical; [23] he suggested that the recurring and me-

[23] This conclusion led Parker to assume that many of the Psalms were composed by some of the rhapsodist prophets.

chanical prefacing formulae, "Thus saith the Lord," has
no special bearing on the technical question of divine inspiration, since this was not thought of by the Hebrews as
being followed by a "special" inspiration.

The conclusions regarding specific textual and critical
problems in the prophetic writings usually follow Eichhorn
and De Wette. The second part of Isaiah, Chapters 40–
66, was assigned to the post-Exilic period; Parker treated
it separately, because of the literary, historical, and formal
unity of the writing. (The distinctions later made between
Chapters 40–55 and 56–66 were not noted by Parker.)
Chapter 13:1–14 and Chapters 23, 35, and 36, were
treated as another separate unit; Chapters 24–27 were
distinguished from the other portions. These conclusions
are noteworthy, because, with De Wette, critics have continued to distinguish between these documents within the
book of Isaiah.

The prophecy of Jeremiah was assigned to the period
between 629 and 588 B.C. Parker dealt with many spurious
passages in this book at greater length than did De Wette;
his criticism regarding the relationship between the Alex-
andrian and the Masoretic versions of Jeremiah is also more
discriminating than was De Wette's. Ezekiel was a book of
prophecy that disappointed Parker. He considered these
utterances as "pseudo-prophetic," because of their "strikingly peculiar priestly spirit," the tedious and repetitious
prose, and the general dullness of the writing. But Parker
admired Ezekiel's powers of observation, some of his descriptions, and several of his "dazzling compositions,"
speaking of him as the "prophetic artist."

In his study of the writings of the twelve minor prophets,
Parker followed De Wette closely; in several technical

questions, he compared De Wette's solutions with those proposed by Eichhorn, Bertholdt, and Maurer. Daniel was more fully dealt with by Parker than by De Wette. His conclusion regarding the textual and exegetical problems of the book was stated as follows:

There seems abundant reason for placing the date of the book in the time of Antiochus Epiphanes (175–160 B.C.) and towards the latter part of his reign . . . The author seems to have written with the design to arouse whatever patriotism and religious feeling was left in their [the Jews'] hearts.[24]

Because this conclusion regarding the dating of Daniel was based on careful critical study, and because this statement of the purpose clearly repudiated the more conservative allegorical interpretations often associated with the book, Parker's viewpoint was advanced for his day.

The treatment of the Hebrew "Writings," though brief, was sensitive to the many literary problems associated with them. The usual distinctions within the poetic books were noted. The Psalms were considered under various categories based on the content of the poems, rather than on their alleged authors. Parker concluded that most of them belong to the Exilic and post-Exilic period, that many were written by the prophets, and that they were compiled for liturgical purposes at a much later date. In his study of the book of Job, which he called "poetic drama," Parker exhibited careful scholarship.

From this survey of some of the most important problems dealt with by Parker in Old Testament criticism we may form a judgment regarding his ability as well as his position as a literary and historical critic. Before we draw our final conclusions, however, it is necessary that we take

[24] *A Critical and Historical Introduction*, pp. 501–502.

into account his study of the New Testament. While he did not study this part of the Bible as extensively, he applied to its documents the same historical and critical methods. De Wette continued to be his favorite guide. In his *Introduction to the Old Testament*, Parker included a chapter on the New Testament. He stated his reason for this clearly: "I intend, at some future date, to prepare an introduction to the New Testament on a similar plan, and this chapter will serve to connect the two." [25] Eichhorn, too, was relied on in his New Testament studies. Parker was particularly attracted by the views of David Friedrich Strauss and Ferdinand Christian Baur, the critical theologians who led the "Tübingen School" of Biblical study.[26] Parker viewed the dogmatic and conservative volumes on New Testament criticism with hesitation; among those works which he rejected as "unscientific" were J. L. Hug's Roman Catholic approach, the German Protestant criticism of H. Olshausen, and the American orthodox Unitarian view of Andrews Norton.[27]

Parker's study of the New Testament as in the case of the Old Testament began with a review of the formation of its canon. He concluded that, during the early centuries of the Christian era, exacting and precise criteria regarding canonicity were followed, but that later leaders of the Church abandoned judgments based on historical accuracy

[25] "Translator's Preface," *op. cit.*, p. x.
[26] Baur's views were elaborated in his major work on *Symbolik und Mythologie* (Tübingen, 1824–25). Strauss' work was entitled *Das Leben Jesu* (Tübingen, 1837); Parker believed it should have been called "A Fundamental Criticism of the Four Gospels." He reviewed it critically in the *Christian Examiner* (April, 1840).
[27] Olshausen's conservative work was translated by David Fosdick in 1838; it was reviewed briefly by Parker in the *Christian Examiner* (July, 1838). Andrews Norton's work was entitled *Evidences for the Genuineness of the Gospels* (Boston, 1837).

and relied primarily on the alleged authorship of the writing. Parker believed that eventually ecclesiastical authority and precedence became the sole criterion for evaluating the canonicity of a given document.

The first problem in the study of the synoptic Gospels was that of interpreting Jesus as a wholly mythological being. Various radical critics and some of the early students of comparative religion had stated the hypothesis that Jesus should be viewed as a non-historical figure. The disciples' vague experiences were emotionally exaggerated and later related in the symbolic language of the Gospel narratives. This was, of course, a radical tendency, but it was not new in the circles of Biblical critics. Herman Samuel Reimarus had proposed such a theory in the early part of the eighteenth century.[28] The Tübingen critics were the first to explore it. Parker accepted the view as an hypothesis, but nevertheless followed the formulations of Baur and Strauss with caution. In the end, he concluded that Jesus was not merely mythical; while the early disciples and the Gospel writers were often swayed by their emotions as they related supposedly historical incidents, the radical position that Jesus was no more than the creation of a "state of mind" could not be accepted. He thus redefined the meaning of "myth" in the Gospels; it is not the same as fantasy, for at its center is an historically verifiable fact. Thus, throughout his critical study of the Gospels, Parker sought to separate "their mythological and legendary narratives from what is purely a matter-of-fact."[29] This, to him, was the most important task of New Testament criticism; textual problems were, by comparison, less

[28] This view, in Reimarus's words, was published by Lessing in the *Wolfenbuttel Fragments* (1777), with which Parker was acquainted.
[29] *A Discourse of Matters Pertaining to Religion*, p. 328.

important.[30] Each of the synoptic Gospels seemed to mingle factual and legendary material; therefore, no one of them could be accepted as historically accurate; and no one could be ascribed precedence over the other two without losing some of the value of the discarded accounts. Critical study, according to Parker, must therefore construct another "picture" of the career of Jesus; it must be based on the materials of the three Gospels after having studied them with the historical and critical tools. A new "gospel" is Parker's goal in synoptic criticism. He summarized his narrative in the following way:

Jesus, a young man full of genius for religion, seems to have begun his public career with the narrow aim of reforming Judaism. He would put all human piety and morality into the venerable forms of Jewish tradition. He came not to destroy but to fulfil the Mosaic law; that was eternal;—his followers were to observe and teach all the customs of the Scribes and Pharisees; the sick man on recovery must offer the Levitical sacrifice. Like John the Baptist he preaches the coming of the Messiah, and the kingdom of heaven. He would not labor for mankind but only for the children of Israel—for it is not meet to give the dogs the children's bread. But as he went on he found his new wine of piety and humanity burst the old wine-skins of Judaism; the old garments which Scribes and Pharisees had inherited from dead prophets could not be patched with new philanthropy, and the nation be thereby clothed withal. He gradually breaks with Judaism, neglects the ceremonial fast, violates the sabbath, speaks evil of the clerical dignities—they are covered pits in the highway, whereinto men fall and perish. He claims himself to be the Messiah; John the Baptist was the Elias who was to come and make ready. He had political plans that lie there indistinctly seen through the mythic cloud which wraps the whole. He reaches beyond Judea to Samaria at least, per-

[30] While he did not assign dates to the Synoptic Gospels, he suggested that Matthew was the first, Mark was second, and Luke, which was based on the other two, was last.

haps to other nations, and develops his religious scheme more freely than at first.[31]

This rewritten Gospel supplied Parker with a reasonable basis for solving what he viewed as the question most troublesome to New Testament criticism—the "synoptic problem." He formulated his earliest understanding of this problem in a very interesting manner:

Do you believe the first three gospel writers got their similarity of fact and language by telling over one story in company so many times that they knew how to put the *otes* and *totes* exactly alike, or do you think that Mark had Matthew before him, and Luke both of them, or how do you fit it! The theory of an *oral gospel* which the noble men learned by heart and repeated when they wanted to tell about the most remarkable man the world ever saw reduces them to a set of *gossiping grannies,* and I can't bear it. Of course I know the literature on this point from Nonnus to Norton—but find a great blur before my eyes when I look at the composition of the four gospels. I know no way to settle the vexed doubt except to "call up him who left untold the story." But this is not critical and I am not *scharfsinnig* enough to solve the puzzle except by supposing one Evangel saw the others' work.[32]

This problem of literary criticism was combined with an historical problem when Parker asked how the synoptic Gospels might be reconciled with the fourth Gospel. An earlier letter to Francis raised a specific problem in this context: "Another question was whether you thought there was any possibility of reconciling the accounts of the time when Christ took the last supper in the Synoptics with that of John? If you can't reconcile them, which do you prefer

[31] *A Discourse of Matters Pertaining to Religion,* pp. 227–228.
[32] Letter to Francis, May 15, 1846; in the possession of the Boston Public Library.

to follow?" [33] Parker proposes a concise solution to the problem as a whole: "The Jesus of the Synoptics differs very widely from the Jesus of John, in his actions, discourses, and general spiritual character, as much as the Socrates of Xenophon from that of Plato." [34]

In regard to the authorship of the four Gospels Parker criticized Strauss for concluding that all are spurious, on the basis of very little proof:

[Strauss] finds little reason for believing the genuineness or the authenticity of the Gospels. Indeed, he regards them all as spurious productions of well-meaning men, who collected the traditions that were current in the part of the world where they respectively lived. This is the weakest part of his book, important as the question is; yet, weak as it is, his chief arguments rest upon it. The proofs of the spuriousness of these books are quite too feeble and uncertain for his purpose.[35]

Though the "genuineness of the Gospels" was a delicate issue in New England during Parker's day, he was inclined to accept Strauss' position and to bolster the latter's evidence by gathering data from other critics as well. Later Parker presented his conclusion: "Here we have, apparently, *though I think not really*, the works of Matthew and John, two of the immediate disciples of Jesus, and of Mark and Luke, the companions of Peter and Paul." [36]

In his study of the incidents connected with Jesus' ministry, Parker followed Strauss closely; this aspect of New Testament study had been emphasized by Strauss in his work. Among Parker's conclusions, with the help of Strauss'

[33] Letter to Francis, November 21, 1840; in the possession of the Boston Public Library.
[34] *A Discourse of Matters Pertaining to Religion*, p. 326.
[35] "Strauss' Life of Jesus," p. 262.
[36] *A Discourse of Matters Pertaining to Religion*, p. 325.

evidence, were these: the miracle stories are unauthentic and represent elaborated "popular" conceptions of the Messiah; Jesus had no foreknowledge of his death and resurrection, and the related "predictions" were written much later; the resurrection has only a "mythical" meaning, since it was unquestionably based on the disciples' belief that the Messiah should live forever. These are, once again, radical and far-reaching conclusions. Parker indicated, independently, a more important critical conjecture. He stated that some of the miracle stories, as well as some of the accounts dealing with the crucifixion and resurrection, were based on early historical fragments, perhaps related to a figure other than Jesus. While he did not expand this conjecture into a theory which stressed the existence of "fragments" in Aramaic, the spoken language of the disciples, which were used later in the writing of the Greek accounts, Parker suggested that such fragments of information must have been available to the Gospel narrators. He also did not relate this conjecture to the "synoptic problem" as later critics have done.

Several other literary and textual questions were raised by Parker. Implications regarding the "pre-existence" of Christ were explored. The intent of the writers of the Gospels in the resurrection narratives was studied carefully. The origins of the sacramental rites of Baptism and the Lord's Supper were looked into. The nature of the primitive Christian community also interested him. On each of these matters, and many others, Parker collected a vast amount of data from many sources.

He was often led to compare Gospel accounts with statements in other New Testament writings. While he was unaware of the textual relationship between the Gospel of

Luke and the book of the Acts of the Apostles, he studied the Acts carefully. He was dissatisfied with the narrative as an accurate historical portrayal and consequently spoke of it as "a mythical and legendary book." The New Testament Epistles were not subjected to such a thorough historical and critical study. Parker concluded that in most cases the alleged authorship of the letters cannot be fully verified, but this generalization did not cause him to discard the opinion of competent scholars that the Epistles are "the earliest Christian documents." From his failure to engage in extensive criticism of the Epistles it may be inferred that they held no great interest for him.[37] He often compared them to the Old Testament prophetic writings, on the ground that in each case the writers did not seem particularly confident that their words were divinely inspired; consequently, Parker referred to the Epistles in arguing against the orthodox view of Biblical inspiration.

Parker's New Testament studies were closely linked with his historical examination of the doctrines of Christian theology. De Wette had given major attention to Christian dogmatics in his earlier years. The Tübingen theologians were also conspicuously represented on Parker's shelves.[38] The products of Baur's scholarship were of special interest to him; the later writings indicated Baur's departure from the early influence of Schleiermacher and his acceptance of an Hegelian methodology. Thus, after 1835, when this shift in his viewpoint occurred, Baur devoted his study almost

[37] Parker's only detailed discussion of the New Testament Epistles was set forth in the *Discourse,* pp. 322–325.
[38] Baur's basic works, in translation, were *The Christian Doctrine of the Atonement* (1838), *The Trinity and the Incarnation* (1841–43), and *Kirchengeschichte* (5 vols., 1853–63). Strauss' fundamental views were stated in *Die Christliche Glaubenslehre* (2 vols., 1841–42).

exclusively to the historical study of Christian dogma. Parker was deeply interested in Baur's critical introduction to the relation of Christian doctrines and the authenticity of the New Testament documents. This, Parker knew, was the distinguishing aspect of Baur's later work in dogmatics. He also included Strauss' *Christliche Glaubenslehre* (1841–42) among his references; this work, according to Parker, best described the Hegelian approach to the history of doctrine. Another work Parker used was the detailed history compiled by Isaac A. Dorner.[39] Though he often referred to it for accurate historical data, Parker was critical of its orthodox viewpoint, charging that Dorner neglected both philosophical and historical methodology in attempting to prove his "main idea . . . that the true Christ is perfect God and perfect man, and that Jesus of Nazareth is the true Christ." [40] Parker also relied heavily on the work of Friedrich August Tholuck, who resembled De Wette closely in his emphasis on philological studies, and on the scholarship of Jacob Sengler, the primary figure in the Marburg School, who developed a theory regarding the evolution of man's idea of God.

In his examination of the history of Christian doctrine, Parker gave his major attention to the fundamental beliefs in God, the relationship between man and God, and immortality. He also centered much of his study on the early dogmas regarding the Church and the Christian sacraments. He included the ethical imperatives of Christianity, evidences for the authority of Jesus, the universal character of inspiration, and the numerous claims for the in-

[39] This history was devoted primarily to Christological doctrines. It appeared in Stuttgart in 1839.
[40] "Thoughts on Theology," a review of Dorner's work; *The Dial* (April, 1842), and *Works*, IV, 210.

fallibility of the Scriptures. Each of these doctrines was examined with considerable care and historical acumen. In general, it was his aim in this historical study to explore fully De Wette's challenge: "If the introduction [to Biblical study] is treated in the genuine scientific spirit of criticism, it has, then, the further advantage of awakening the spirit of historical investigation in theology." [41] The historical study of doctrine was, therefore, closely related to his use of critical tools in the study of the Bible; the one logically accompanied the other.

Parker also saw that his historical criticism had practical and prophetic implications. Later in his life, his idealistic interpretation of Jesus became a basis for his ambitions in moral reform. His "picture" of Jesus supported his faith in a progressive view of history. It revealed to him the inherent possibilities for perfection in all men; they were clearly developed in the person of Jesus: "I thank God for the history which Jesus is! I thank him more for the prophecy which he is!" [42] His study of the primitive Christian community stimulated his interest in reforming the Church from within. Parker did not follow the course of many of his colleagues in resigning from the ministry; he aimed rather, through remaining in the Church, at an internal transformation of its purpose and nature. He concluded that much of the institutional character of the Church needed to be destroyed; it often impoverished and tyrannized mankind. It could eventually become a true community of men who love God and one another; since in its founding the Church had been established as a spontaneous, loving community, so it could again approximate this ideal.

[41] *A Critical and Historical Introduction*, I, 5.
[42] *Views of Religion* (Boston, 1885), p. 281.

It is clear that Parker's critical and historical erudition in
the Bible and Christian dogmatics had practical ends in
view.

This is, nevertheless, not the only conclusion we can
draw. It is important for our study to estimate Parker's
stature as a critic and with respect to other American
critics. Our first impression may be a valid one: Parker was
primarily a popularizer of critical study. He did not ini-
tiate significant new critical formulations. His conclusions
were usually based on the arguments cited by other scholars.
His importance is not found in his ability as a creative
scholar. He relied for his judgments on the evidence which
had been collected by others. His edition of De Wette's
Einleitung was a remarkable work. Of it, a reviewer wrote
in the *Christian Examiner:*

Few, even among scholars, can easily reckon the amount of
labor bestowed by the translator. For anything except the mere
critical reference he has made it is practically a new work. The
whole body of literature which it reflects and represents, he has
studied with independent judgment, posting up the bibliography of the subject to the freshest dates. . . . He fairly
divides the honors with the original composer; . . . this
striking monument to his dogged industry and scholarly wealth
of reading we take pleasure in welcoming to its permanent place
among the classics of Biblical criticism.[43]

Despite this praise, Parker's work did not constitute a
creative contribution to Biblical scholarship; it was, rather,
a critical review of the literature and the significant conclusions of others. When he dealt with technical questions,
he usually followed De Wette's conjectures, leaving De
Wette only to rely on some other competent scholar. No-
where in the *Introduction* is there a significant example of

[43] *Christian Examiner* (October, 1843), p. 73.

Parker's completely independent critical judgment. Even in his study of the New Testament, where his criticism is almost entirely confined to the Gospels, his conclusions were, in general, modifications and revisions of earlier work.

Nevertheless, he was among the first in America to conceive of Biblical criticism as a field of scientific inquiry. He was a prophet of historical criticism in the New World. He was one of the first to be convinced that Biblical study should be pursued in the truly scientific spirit, and that it should employ the shining tools of the scientist. He believed, furthermore, that such a critical approach could make acceptable a new view of the Scriptures which would then revolutionize the Church. He was a radical in America in his belief that among the most important and necessary steps in theological study was the thorough rejection of the claims of Scriptural infallibility.

The early Edwardian theology of the Westminster Confession had no interest in Biblical study from the viewpoint of historical criticism. It conceived of the Scriptures as "the rule of faith and practice" and looked to its pages only for proof-texts. William Ellery Channing's later pattern of Biblical exegesis appeared to favor the critical approach. In his elaborate exposition of Unitarianism in the historic "Baltimore Sermon," Channing outlined the principles to be adopted in Scriptural interpretation and listed the doctrines which could be stated on the basis of this interpretation. He expressed the necessity of understanding fully the historical context of any given passage, the general purpose of the writer, and the peculiarities of the language. But Channing's approach was essentially conservative; he explained contradictions in the Bible on non-scientific grounds.

We ought, indeed, to expect occasional obscurity in such a book as the Bible, which was written for the past and future ages as well as the present. But God's wisdom is a pledge that whatever is necessary for *us,* and necessary for salvation, is revealed too plainly to be mistaken, and too consistently to be questioned, by a sound and upright mind.[44]

This explains why Channing often questioned Parker's revolutionary approach.

The view of Biblical study set forth by Moses Stuart of Andover was still more orthodox than Channing's. Stuart has, nevertheless, been repeatedly referred to as "the father of Biblical learning in this country." [45] His essential conclusion is clearly stated: "I believe that the Scriptures reveal the facts." [46] He adhered to this creed throughout his studies, which on the whole were considered erudite and competent. To Stuart, Christian dogmas were of greater significance than historical criticism; he was not inclined to subject the Bible to examination with scientific tools. Furthermore, he thought of his learning as a means of supporting the validity of orthodox doctrines.

Andrews Norton is comparable to Stuart in all respects. Edward Robinson must also be included as belonging to this school of learning. While Henry Ware held a similar viewpoint, he often opposed Stuart, but advised his students at Harvard to follow the Bible if their own personal views differed with the revealed truth. The Universalists also had their scholars of the Bible; they, like the orthodox Unitarians, set forth the theory of Biblical "evidences." Hosea Ballou showed little interest in such evidence for his

44 Channing, *Works* (Boston, 1875), p. 370.
45 Frank Hugh Foster, *A Genetic History of the New England Theology* (Chicago, 1907), p. 289.
46 Moses Stuart, *Letters* (1846), p. 23.

arguments for universal salvation: "I am determined to admit no Scripture as evidence in this case that needs an interpretation to cause it to mean what I wish to prove: therefore I shall produce but a small part of the Scriptures which I conceive have a direct meaning in favor of Universalism." [47]

Walter Balfour, who gave expression to a more exegetical form of the doctrine central to Universalism, was more competent than Ballou with respect to Biblical scholarship. His understanding of Hebrew and Greek was valuable in his involved interpretations of the temporal implications of such concepts as "Sheol," "Hades," "Gehenna" and "Hell," but he finally concluded that no characteristic Biblical word conveys the meaning of endless suffering.

Nathaniel Emmons, the Hopkinsian Calvinist, entered into the dispute between Universalists and the orthodox clergy, and he sought on the basis of Biblical study to discredit the Universalists' position. Emmons' dogmatic approach to Scriptural exegesis was supported by his theological views. He advocated the position that the interpretation of Scripture must begin with certain "first principles" and that such principles can be found among the fundamental doctrines of Christian theology.

No doctrine can be proved or refuted by merely marshalling one class of texts against another without explaining them according to some sound and accepted principle. Texts ought never to be adduced to explain and establish any first principles; but first principles are to be adduced to explain and establish the sense of every text of Scripture.[48]

[47] Hosea Ballou, *A Treatise on Atonement* (4th ed., Boston, 1882), p. 236.
[48] Nathaniel Emmons, *Works*, V, 599.

The leaders in the "New England theology" held similarly dogmatic views. Emmons was one of its spokesmen. Another one was Leonard Woods, who was among the first to give strictly academic lectures in systematic theology in New England in the nineteenth century. He was the first professor of Systematic Theology at Andover Theological Seminary. Because this seminary had been formed by the union of two parties in the evangelical wing of Congregationalism—the "moderate" Calvinists and the Hopkinsians —Woods made both the Westminster Confession and a separate creed of the second group the foundations for his system. Thus, the Scriptures were taken as the last authority for the doctrines which he systematized; in his "Lectures," Woods maintained that the Bible was inspired, that it is therefore free from error, and that specific interpretations as set forth by his colleague, Moses Stuart, are final.[49] The theological position of Timothy Dwight at Yale was in general agreement; "evidences" for final validity could, he said, be taken from the Bible. This authoritative view of the Scriptures was also maintained by the New England Presbyterians. Enoch Pond of Bangor agreed in its fundamentals with the doctrinal system of the New England evangelical theology. He argued for Biblical authority on the basis of the witness of the Holy Spirit.

I have but another argument to urge in favor of the divine authority of the Bible—the same which was urged in support of its truth; it is that which the Christian finds in his own soul. . . . [True Christians] find such a blessed agreement between the representations of Scripture and the feelings of their own hearts that they cannot doubt as to the divine origin of the Bible. It must have proceeded from the same Being who knows the hearts of his children perfectly. . . . This argument has more weight, probably, than every other, with Christians in common life, to

49 See Leonard Woods, *Works,* I, 95ff.

remove their doubts and give them a settled, unwavering faith in the truth and divine authority of the sacred word.[50]

Despite what has been said about Woods's "Lectures," no fully developed system of Christian theology appeared in New England until one was formulated by Edwards A. Park. He attempted, in his statement of the theological doctrines, to remain abreast of the developments in Biblical study. He did not concern himself with the technical aspects of textual and historical criticism, but on several occasions he altered his theological views on the basis of new discoveries in Biblical criticism. He stated that it was his aim to prove the validity of Christian dogmas by using first the method of natural theology as elaborated by Paley, and by appealing secondly to the "Biblical arguments." He conceived of the Bible as "a part of natural theology," though he hesitated to relinquish his belief that it must be accorded final and supreme authority. According to Park, the Bible is a book of wisdom which presents an entire system of knowledge, and because it teaches the benevolence of God, it must be true. Thus, Christianity was taught as *the* Biblical religion; its doctrines derive their first and final proof from the revealed Scriptures. Park interpreted Scriptural inspiration as having applicability only to the writers of the Biblical documents; thus, the writings are not inspired as writings. He suggested a "divine superintendency" over the writers, so that they were at all times in accord with God's will. What they wrote is therefore true on the basis of divine revelation. This is Park's implicit criticism of the scientific method of critical study. More explicit was his charge that since neither scientific nor historical truth is recorded in the Bible, neither scientific nor historical means can be applied to the documents with final validity. These

[50] Enoch Pond, *Lectures on Christian Theology* (Boston, 1867), p. 120.

were criticisms which supported Park's view that the miracles recorded in the Bible need little evidence to prove their occurrence, since the *occasion* for their happening is always present in the Biblical accounts.

Thus, the viewpoint prevalent among Biblical and theological scholars during Parker's day was, on the whole, conservative and dogmatic. The critical approach as represented by De Wette, Baur, and Strauss was not generally welcomed, and Parker's work based on their views was not received sympathetically. Only a limited number of his colleagues, particularly Convers Francis, accepted, as a major contribution, Parker's amplification of De Wette's historical approach. Most of the scholars who reviewed the work agreed with Moses Stuart, that "De Wette, with all his talent and learning (and he has much of both), is a very hasty, and not infrequently a very inaccurate writer, and is not always to be depended on where long continued and patient research must be made." [51] The critics supported their opposition by detailed technical arguments. Both Stuart and Noyes, who together opposed the historical method, voiced their dissatisfaction with many of the specific conclusions Parker had drawn from Eichhorn and De Wette; contrasting opinions were stated, and personal conclusions were forcefully expressed.[52]

Parker's ideal and characteristic approach to the problems of textual and historical criticism stands apart from the others that have been cited. He was not a creative and independent critic. But he was radical in his position regarding the strictly scientific character of critical study.

[51] Moses Stuart, Review Article in *The Biblical Repository,* No. XXV (April, 1839), p. 331.
[52] These reviews appeared in both *The Biblical Repository* and the *Bibliotheca Sacra.*

He forcefully opposed the attempts to retain the authoritative position of the Bible. He was disturbed even by Strauss'
conservative conclusion that "the germ of Christian faith
is entirely independent of critical investigations." [53] Thus,
if Parker holds an important position in the history of Biblical criticism in America, it is primarily because he consistently treated the Biblical documents with scientific,
historical, and critical methods, conceiving these methods
as wholly valid for the formulation of "educated" conclusions about the Bible as a whole as well as for its doctrinal
content. Parker was the American prophet for the acceptance of the Bible as an historical product. He was among
the first in America to face squarely its numerous errors
and contradictions. He recognized many of the errors made
by copyists as they misread the Hebrew consonants, mis-
placed or omitted letters, words, or passages, and noted
many others made by scribes who had misunderstood the
reading of the original documents. He noted that other
errors resulted from the conscious changes made by editors
or the early Masoretic textual redactors; he was also cog-
nizant of some errors which were made as a result of changes
in the manuscript to adapt the document to a new historical
setting. These and other reasons, with many illustrations,
were added by Parker in a special section in his edition of
the *Introduction* which was devoted to "Biblical errors."
De Wette had not touched on this matter; that Parker felt
called on to discuss the errors is especially significant in
view of the fact that other critics in America were silent on
the subject.

In his *Introduction*, Parker repeatedly contrasted his
view of the universal scope of divine inspiration and the

[53] Strauss, *Das Leben Jesu*, I, 12.

narrow and limited claims made by those critics who viewed the Bible as the infallible source of theological doctrines, and as the book which forever closed the process of divine inspiration. For his part, the writers of the Biblical documents made no pretense of infallibility, and that, therefore, the dogmatic position based on "special" revelations is untenable. He continuously placed in juxtaposition his favorite critical scholars whom he spoke of as "scientists" and those critics whom he called "blind and undiscriminating," because they made "*dogmatic theology* . . . the touchstone wherewith we are to decide between the true and the false, the genuine and the spurious." [54] In a letter to Francis, he wrote,

the main difference between us and the orthodox is not respecting the doctrine of the trinity, or total depravity, or the fall, or election (for we all agree near enough on these points and believe in "God the Father," in revelations *in* man, which *is* the *Son,* and revelations *to* man, which *is the Holy Spirit*), but in respect to the Scriptures. The orthodox places the Bible above the soul, we the soul above the Bible.[55]

Thus, one of his aims was to destroy the orthodox view of the Bible. He believed that bibliolatry was Protestantism's most flagrant sin. The unenlightened dogmatism of the orthodox system was its greatest error. Theological reform became his goal. Throughout his life he believed that

criticism—which the thinking character of the age demands—asks men to do consciously and thoroughly what they have always done imperfectly and with no science but that of a pious heart; that is, to divide the word rightly, separate mythology from history, fact from fiction, what is religious and of God, from what is earthly and not of God; to take the Bible for what it is worth. . . . .

[54] *A Critical and Historical Introduction,* I, 4.
[55] Letter to Francis, February 9, 1839; in the possession of the Boston Public Library.

This doctrine takes nothing from the Bible but its errors; its truth remains, brilliant and burning with the light of life. . . . The Bible was made for man, not man for the Bible.[56]

That we know so little of the authorship of the biblical books is fatal to their authority as a standard of faith, but it does not in the smallest degree affect their value as religious documents. . . . They are monuments of the various ages, though we know not who made or put them together.[57]

Parker's was not an early and merely fleeting interest in critical study; he never abandoned this interest. He was neither wholly distracted by reform, nor was he "converted" to a more transcendentalist viewpoint because of having become disillusioned about his ability to command in contemporaries like Emerson a serious respect for critical and historical study. It is true that fifteen years of his later life were devoted to an intensive participation in programs of reform, but even during this period he merged the academic aims of his Biblical study with more practical, prophetic, or "sermonic" purposes.

Our conclusion regarding Parker's Biblical scholarship is, therefore, threefold. His early contributions were not significant for their originality. Though he was respected for his radical conclusions, he was not welcomed as the expounder of new theories. He was, however, a great advocate and preacher of criticism, and the foremost American prophet of "scientific" Biblical learning. His criticism was not cultivated merely for scholarly ends; he thought of it as a vital step in religious, as well as social, reform. The most technical research seemed to him also intensely practical.

[56] *A Discourse of Matters Pertaining to Religion,* pp. 333, 336, and 341.
[57] "The Conception of God in the Bible," *Works,* VI, 103.

Chapter 3

THE RELIGIOUS ELEMENT IN
HUMAN NATURE

PARKER'S INTEREST in critical problems in the field of dogmatics did not constitute the whole of his theological studies. Nor did his opposition to orthodox views end with his historical study of the Bible. The formulation of a philosophy of religion that would adequately interpret the nature of religious knowledge was a concern central to his theological scholarship. His views on the relation of religion to human nature were initially expressed during a controversy among New England transcendentalists and theologians that was most intense between 1839 and 1845.

Emerson set off the controversy when, on Sunday evening, July 15, 1838, he delivered his "Divinity School Address" to members of the faculty, alumni, and theological students. He had already become known to a wide circle of his contemporaries. His "first authentic utterance," [1] the booklet on *Nature*, was already being regarded by many as the "most complete presentation of transcendentalism." [2] The address of 1838 was directly continuous with his earlier expressions of transcendentalist doctrine. He continued to assume that the role of reason is of highest sig-

[1] Edwin D. Mead, *The Influence of Emerson* (Boston, 1903), p. 12.
[2] Kenneth W. Cameron, *Emerson the Essayist* (Raleigh, N.C., 1945), I, 200.

nificance in man's perception of individual spiritual truths, whereas the role of the understanding is by comparison of minor importance. "There is no doctrine of the Reason," said Emerson, "which will bear to be taught by the understanding." [3] He also reaffirmed his belief in the beauty of nature, the supreme authority of "spiritual laws," and the sentiment of human virtue. "Good is positive. . . . Benevolence is absolute and real. . . . This sentiment is divine and deifying. . . . Through it, the soul knows itself . . . [and] then [man] can worship, and be enlarged by his worship, for he can never go behind this sentiment." [4] The key words of transcendentalism were already underscored: "sentiment," "the soul," and "worship." The address then launched into an extended criticism of the Unitarian clergy, who, Emerson said, had lost creative inspiration and spontaneous faith. He charged them with preaching only from "memory" or traditions, not from the soul. "In the soul let redemption be sought." "Miracles, prophecy, poetry, the ideal life, the holy life, exist as ancient history merely; they are not in the belief, nor in the aspiration, of society." [5] Still more specific was his criticism that the church repeatedly corrupted the "miracle" by turning it into a "monster." Instead of following Jesus' belief that "man's life was a miracle," the church profaned the individual soul by "converting a man by miracles." [6] The essence of the individualistic gospel of self-reliance was implicit in these criticisms. He was contrasting the church with the soul; he stated the need for preaching a "new revelation"—the human soul—whose truths are to be trusted because they are intuitive and direct. He asserted that man can and

[3] Ralph Waldo Emerson, *The Divinity School Address* (Boston, 1838), pp. 7–8.
[4] *Ibid.*, pp. 4–5. [5] *Ibid.*, p. 7. [6] *Ibid.*, p. 10.

must love God without having to rely on evidences external to the soul.

This new gospel fell into the stiff and proper camp of the New England clergy with the reverberations of a thunderbolt. Henry Ware, Jr., promptly informed Emerson of the Harvard Unitarians' displeasure. In reply, Emerson wrote:

what you say about the Discourse . . . is just what I might expect from your truth and charity combined with your known opinions. "I am not a stock or a stone" as one said in the old time, and could not but feel pain in saying some things in that place and presence where I supposed they might meet dissent —and the dissent, I may say, of dear friends and benefactors of mine. Yet, as my conviction is perfect in the substantial truth of the doctrine, and is not very new, you will see at once that it must appear to me very important that it be spoken out, and I thought I would not pay the nobleness of my friends so mean a compliment as to suppress any opposition to their supposed views out of fear of offence. I would rather say to them, these things look so to me; to you otherwise; let us say out our uttermost word, and let the all-prevailing Truth, as it surely will, judge between us. We shall either of us I doubt not be equally glad to be apprised of the error. Meantime I shall be admonished by this expression of your thought to revise with greater care the manuscript before it is printed (for the use of the class), and I heartily thank you for this renewed expression of your kind toleration and love.[7]

Ware's comments were only a slight prelude to the storm about to break. Apparently every man in Emerson's audience was stirred to protest. The line of attack varied, but it was obvious that the Unitarians were divided into two chief camps. Parker commented on the division in a letter to George W. Ellis: "It is quite evident that there are now two parties among the Unitarians; one is for progress, the

[7] Letter, July 28, 1838, *The Letters of Ralph Waldo Emerson*, II, 148–150.

other says, 'Our strength is to stand still.' Dr. Channing is
the real head of the first party; the other has no head. . . .
Some day or another there will be a rent in the body." [8]
Andrews Norton assumed the position of "head" for the
opposition, becoming a sort of "high priest" of the orthodox group. He was the first to give a detailed criticism of
Emerson's assertions. In an address given a year later than
Emerson's and called "A Discourse on the Latest Form of
Infidelity," Norton charged his predecessor with having
recklessly assaulted the foundation of the Christian religion. The dispute was immediately narrowed down to a
specific matter when he made this idea his central thesis:
"if there are no miracles, there is no religion."

No proof of [Christ's] divine commission could be afforded but
through miraculous displays of God's power. Nothing is left
that can be called Christianity, if its miraculous character be
denied. Its essence is gone; its evidence is annihilated. . . .
There can be no intuition, no direct perception, of the truth of
Christianity, no metaphysical certainty.[9]

Though Norton stated his position forcefully, he failed
to buttress it by means of his New Testament studies regarding the "genuineness" of the Gospel accounts and his
unhesitating belief that the slightest Biblical evidence is
authoritative. Instead, he evaded the issue and made a dogmatic attack on "the new German theology." He declared
that Spinoza, De Wette, Schleiermacher, and Strauss occu-
pied chief positions in this new school. "The celebrated
atheist, Spinoza" was included because he was "the first
writer . . . who maintained the impossibility of a miracle;

---

[8] Letter to Ellis, January 3, 1839, quoted by John Weiss, *The Life and
Correspondence of Theodore Parker*, I, 119.
[9] Andrews Norton, *A Discourse on the Latest Form of Infidelity*,
(Cambridge, 1839), pp. 22 and 32.

. . . [this] denial must involve the denial of the existence of God." [10] De Wette was attacked for believing
that

the new rational theology must accomplish the solution of the
problem of producing a living recognition of faith in its independence of metaphysical and historical knowledge . . . not
resting the truth of Christian faith, as if it were a duty so to do,
upon common, naked, historical truth. Especially let us re-
nounce what has hitherto been customary, the poor and
unscientific appeal to miraculous evidence.[11]

Norton believed that Schleiermacher's basic error was his
elaboration of

a system of pantheism . . . [in which] religion is the sense of
the union of the individual with the universe, with Nature, or, in
the language of the sect, with the One and All; it is a feeling; it
has nothing to do with belief or action . . . ; it is independent
of the idea of a personal God; . . . and the belief and desire of
personal immortality are "wholly irreligious." [12]

D. F. Strauss, according to Norton's view, carried to their
logical extremes the conclusions of "the new theology," for
he separated completely the rational from the supernatural,
thereby "undermining Christianity . . . [rather] than
providing a stable foundation for anything proposed." [13]
The entire "new theology" was criticized for having made
the fundamental assertion

that religion arises out of the nature of man; that it is a feeling,
a sentiment, an apprehension of something, it is hard to say
what, that is intuitive or spontaneous, though admitting of

[10] *Ibid.,* pp. 9 and 11.
[11] This is Norton's translation of a passage from De Wette's article
in Ulmann and Umbreit, *Theologische Studien und Kritiken,* No. 1
(1834), pp. 151–152.
[12] Norton based this view of Schleiermacher on the lectures *Über Religion;* Norton's comment is quoted from his *Discourse,* pp. 43–44.
[13] *Ibid.,* p. 48.

cultivation. . . . [This] theology has allied itself with atheism, with pantheism, and with the other irreligious speculations that have appeared in those metaphysical systems from which the God of Christianity is excluded.[14]

By these charges, Norton had, at least momentarily, shifted the center of the debate; he believed, however, that the fundamental doctrines of the new theology were closely related to Emerson's "new revelation."

The problems which Norton had raised—the authoritative value of the miracles, and the entire issue of the basis for religious knowledge—were questions which others soon explored more fully. In a detailed reply, George Ripley noted that Norton had failed to distinguish between the denial of Christianity's divine origin and the denial of the New Testament miracles. A defense, based primarily on criticisms of Norton's translations of Spinoza, Schleiermacher, and De Wette made up the bulk of the reply, which demonstrated a predominantly philological interest. The criticisms Norton had leveled against Strauss were completely ignored.[15]

Parker had already become deeply interested in the controversy. In his opinion, the central point was being missed: "there is a higher word to be said on this subject than Ripley is disposed to say just now." [16] And Parker prepared to say it. He underscored first what he believed to be the significant question: Why do men have religious beliefs and aspirations? A second question followed: Why are the fundamental expressions of religion similar in the various historical forms of religion? These questions involved an

14 *Ibid.*, pp. 10 and 49.
15 See George Ripley, *Letters on the Latest Form of Infidelity* (Boston, 1840), p. 23ff.
16 Quoted from Parker's *Journal;* John Chadwick, *Theodore Parker, Preacher and Reformer*, p. 92.

entire philosophy, which he felt competent to outline. Among his resources were his Biblical studies, a knowledge of the historical development of Christian theology, and an unusually extensive acquaintance with the best scholarship in the historical study of religions. His West Roxbury congregation realized that in addition to his simple piety, Parker possessed a diversity of interest and knowledge. And, he had already given them a "prospectus" of his position.[17] That position was not widely known, however, outside the immediate community until he entered the controversy; thereafter he became, in some respects, the center of the controversy itself.[18] He issued three manifestoes containing his initial views (1) the pseudonymous letter of 1840, usually referred to as the "Levi Blodgett Letter"; [19] (2) the "South Boston Sermon" of May 19, 1841, which he entitled "The Transient and the Permanent in Christianity"; [20] and (3) the five lectures given during the winter of 1841 and 1842, at the invitation of a group of the leading citizens of Boston and on the urgent counsel of Charles

[17] The sermon which he intended to have serve this purpose was entitled "The Relation of the Bible to the Soul." He preached it on Sunday, April 21, 1839. It was reprinted in the *Western Messenger* (December, 1840, and January, 1841). It is available in *Works,* IV, 58–75. Several of the sermons in his volume entitled *West Roxbury Sermons* (Boston, 1902) are also relevant to this purpose, illustrating well how Parker developed his views in the humble surroundings of his West Roxbury parish.

[18] Emerson had dropped out of the controversy; his correspondence and Journals written during this time indicate no interest on his part in the progress of the controversy.

[19] The full title of this letter follows: *The Previous Question between Mr. Andrews Norton and His Alumni, Moved and Handled in a Letter to All Those Gentlemen,* by Levi Blodgett (Boston, 1840). Because so few copies of this letter are available, and because it was not reprinted in the centenary edition of Parker's *Works,* the Appendix to this volume contains a reprint in full.

[20] See Parker's *Works,* IV, 1–39.

Ellis, and published as *A Discourse of Matters Pertaining to Religion.*[21]

These three works express Parker's earliest and somewhat systematic philosophy of religion. They form one unit with respect to his fundamental affirmations. The "Levi Blodgett Letter" stated clearly what Parker thought of as the central question of the controversy: "How do men come to have any religion, or, in other words, *on what evidence do they receive the plainest religious truths?*" [22] He called this "the previous question" and his answer was stated in several ways. The orthodox answers were discarded, for Parker was convinced that the miracles cannot be interpreted as evidence for the truth of Christian doctrines.

I believe that Jesus, like other religious teachers, wrought miracles. . . . But I see not how a miracle proves a doctrine.

I allow there is a vein of the miraculous pervading human history. . . . But it is a difficult matter to establish a particular miracle.[23]

Now if it could be shown that Christianity rested on miracles, or had more or less connection with them, it yet proves nothing peculiar in the case, for other forms of religions, fetichistic, polytheistic, and monotheistic, appeal to the same authority. If a nation is rude and superstitious, the claim to miracles is the more common; their authority is the greater. . . .

Now in resting Christianity on this basis we must do one of two things: either, first, we must admit that Christianity rests on the same foundation with the lowest fetichism, but has less divine authority than that, for if miracles constitute the

21 This work has appeared in many editions. Parker's latest (Boston, 1856), which is the basis for the edition in his *Works,* Vol. I, contains valuable notes which Parker added. It also shows extensive revision over the earliest edition; Parker said that changes had been made to bring the volume up to date "in the light of the theological science of the present day."

22 *Levi Blodgett Letter,* p. 140 of this work.   23 *Ibid.,* pp. 154 and 155.

authority, then that is the best form of religion which counts the most miracles; or, secondly, we must deny the reality of all miracles except the Christian, in order to give exclusive sway to Christianity.[24]

Two principles emerge as significant in Parker's position regarding the authoritative value of miracles. The first is that, though the miracles could be proved as historical occurrences, still they could be given no value as evidence for the truth of theological doctrines. It is of interest that Parker eventually abandoned his early belief that Jesus performed miracles; after having studied the Gospels critically, he said, "I think they cannot be admitted as facts. . . . I cannot believe such monstrous facts on such evidence." [25] The second principle was based on the history of religions. He momentarily accepted Norton's position regarding miraculous proofs and then turned it upon itself: if Christianity bases its truth on miracles, then it is not unique or "special" truth; Christian theology then has no more validity than the doctrines of religions which it would deem "pagan." Once miraculous evidence is admitted, the most primitive and rude of fetichistic superstitions are the more abundantly validated. The alternative is to follow the course of dogmatism and admit the authority and validity of the Christian miracles only.

Having rejected, therefore, the argument for Christian truth based on the miracles, Parker examined a second position within orthodoxy—the truth of Christianity based on the divinity of Christ. He concluded that this too is an insufficient argument:

it seems difficult to conceive any reason why moral and religious truths should rest for their support on the personal authority of

24 *A Discourse of Religion*, pp. 241–242.   25 *Ibid.*, p. 248.

their revealer, any more than the truths of science on that of him who makes them known first or most clearly. It is hard to see why the great truths of Christianity rest on the personal authority of Jesus, more than the axioms of geometry rest on the personal authority of Euclid or Archimedes. The authority of Jesus . . . must rest on the truth of his words, and not their truth on his authority.[26]

Parker stated his position still more fully by referring to the conclusions of the Tübingen theologians in their New Testament studies. Equally important was his reference to the critical and historical conclusions of Old and New Testament scholars as he rejected the orthodox arguments which based Christian theology on the infallible and inspired Scriptures. This was his negative conclusion: the validity of Christian doctrines cannot be proven by references either to the miracles, the divinity of Christ, or the Scriptures.

These negative answers to his "previous question" did not, however, signify to Parker that the Christian doctrines have no validity. But he believed that such authority must be sought in another area: a comprehensive and critical methodology should be established and then be used to determine the truth of religious teachings. Thus, the elaboration of his methodology forms an important part of his views in the philosophy of religion. His characteristic methodology was made up of two interrelated aspects of inquiry. He used various terms to describe his methods. First, we must examine "the primitive facts of consciousness" [27] and, secondly, offer "proof [of them] experimentally by . . . history." [28] Later in his career he stated it in other words: "the science of theology will be based on

26 "The Transient and Permanent in Christianity," pp. 17–18.
27 "Experience as a Minister," p. 302. 28 Levi Blodgett Letter, p. 143.

facts of observation and facts of consciousness." [29] By "facts of consciousness," Parker meant those facts which can be determined by an analytical examination of human nature, or by what he called "the intuition of [or "into"] human nature." [30] "Facts of observation," on the other hand, are those arrived at by the scientific study of human experience in history. His approach, therefore, was an attempt to

take both the method of the natural philosopher, who looks on things in large masses, gathers from a wide field of observation, and by many facts connects what is exceptional, extra, or deficient, in a single case; and . . . the method of the metaphysician who studies the facts of his own individual consciousness, and gathers his knowledge from that little walled-garden of private experience.[31]

He conceived of his methodology as combining the kind of inquiry engaged in by the "reflective" philosopher with that which is characteristic of the "scientific" or "natural" philosopher. In the introductory paragraphs of his essay on "Transcendentalism," Parker attempted to outline the method and the problem of philosophy.

Now in the pursuit of philosophy there are two methods which may be followed, namely, the deductive and the inductive.

By the deductive, the philosopher takes a certain maxim or principle, assumes it as a fact and therefrom deduces certain other maxims or principles as conclusions, as facts.

[29] "False and True Theology," a sermon preached in Boston, on Sunday, February 14, 1848; *Works*, IV, 358.
[30] *A Discourse of Religion*, p. 10.
[31] "The Innermost Facts of Religious Consciousness," the first in a series of sermons which Parker called "God's Revelation in Matter and Mind"; these sermons were given in November, 1857, and in January, 1858. The quotation above is from *Works*, VI, 234.

By the inductive method the philosopher takes facts, puts them together after a certain order, seen in nature or devised in his own mind, and tries to find . . . a *law*.

In the deductive method you pass from a universal fact to a particular fact; in the inductive, from the particular to the general.

The problem of philosophy [*is*] to explain the facts of the universe; such the two departments of philosophy, physics and metaphysics; such the two methods of inquiry, deductive and inductive. . . . The problem of metaphysics [is] to explain the facts of human consciousness.[32]

This description is helpful in our understanding of Parker's twofold methodology. He believed that "facts of consciousness," or facts that are arrived at through the deductive method, are universals, which must then be used as principles in order to determine particulars. "Facts of observation" are, on the other hand, those "facts" which are inductively arrived at, and are particulars which can be employed in order to discover universals. Thus, the two aspects of his methodology are complementary; each has its basic limitations, but these limitations are overcome when the other half of the method is employed. And, finally, the duality in method is reflected by a fundamental duality in the problems with which philosophy deals.

The fact that Parker accorded equal and complementary importance to "facts of observation" and "facts of consciousness" is characteristic of his scholarship. He saw no

32 "Transcendentalism," an essay or discourse, about which little is known. Because it supplements material which he outlined in his sermons on the "Theological and Philosophical Development of New England," this essay may belong to the same general period, i.e., about 1850. The essay was first published by the Free Tract Society on February 1, 1876; for a reprint, see *Works*, Vol. VI; the quotations have been taken from pp. 3, 4, 6, and 7.

contradiction between his inquiry into "the primitive facts of consciousness" and his "systematic ransacking [of] the facts of history with the tools of science." [33] Nor did it appear contradictory to him that he should devote himself to "massive learning" and wide reading in a privately gathered collection of great books, while he was at the same time seeking to determine the "facts of consciousness." Each process, according to his view, formed half of a total approach in scholarly learning. And, with respect to religion, Parker devoted his study to the examination of religion in its relation to human nature, and secondly in its relation to human history.

Through his systematic study of human nature, Parker discovered empirical evidence for the fact of consciousness which he spoke of as "the religious element in human nature." [34] One cannot easily determine what was meant by the phrase. His further descriptions are consistently vague. He made references to "the religious faculty," without distinguishing it clearly from other "spiritual" faculties. When he called it an "instinct," he obviously meant an emotional rather than a biological fact in human nature. In his *Levi Blodgett Letter*, where his language was for good reason circumspect, he spoke of the religious element as a "germ," a "fact of nature," or as "the religious sentiment . . . born in man." [35] The meaning which he often attached to the phrase is clarified somewhat by his repeated references to his position as the direct opposite of the orthodox view that religion must be based on authorities or influences

[33] Henry Steele Commager, "The Dilemma of Theodore Parker," *The New England Quarterly* (June, 1933). Professor Commager maintained, in this article, that Parker's dilemma was precisely this dual approach to factual data.
[34] *A Discourse of Religion*, p. 4 ff.   [35] *Levi Blodgett Letter*, p. 141.

external to man. What his phrase implied was, therefore, that religious truths must be grounded in man's nature. He said that religion belongs to "the ontology of man"; as he studied human nature, he became convinced that "religion . . . comes out of a principle, deep and permanent in the constitution of man." [36] He therefore maintained that the religious element is a "foundation-element" in man, and that "man is by nature a religious being, i.e., that he was made to be religious." [37]

While these statements help to clarify Parker's purpose in speaking of "the religious element in human nature," it is true that his terminology is essentially obscure. This is so, particularly, in his use of the term "intuition." He said that Kant suggested to him the methodology whereby he "found certain great primal intuitions of human nature, which depend on no logical process of demonstration, but are rather facts of consciousness given by the instinctive action of human nature itself; [the] first is the instinctive intuition of the divine." [38]

René Wellek has pointed out that this was a misinterpretation of the Kantian method,[39] and that Parker had obviously been greatly influenced by Charles Follen's description of the transcendental categories as "innate ideas." Various indications suggest that Parker's "intuition" may be translated "reason." He used both words to describe man's immediate, or spontaneous, spiritual consciousness. This implies a distinct difference between the direct approach to spiritual truths and the Kantian "practical"

---

[36] *A Discourse of Religion*, p. 4.
[37] *Levi Blodgett Letter*, p. 140.
[38] "Experience as a Minister," pp. 301–302.
[39] See René Wellek's article on "The Minor Transcendentalists and German Philosophy," p. 669,

reason.[40] Parker did not conceive of this inner assurance of truth as the empirical discovery of spiritual entities as supersensuous objects. He said, for example, that both God and his own existence are "certainties"; but the latter is determined on the basis of sensuous awareness, while "the idea of God" is a judgment: "The idea of God, like that of liberty and immortality may be called a *judgment a priori*, and from the necessity of the case, transcends all objective experience, as it is logically anterior to it." [41] The role of the reason or of intuition is as a court of final appeal, the voice of ultimate sanction. The reason utters "judgments." And, such judgments are made with respect to "concepts" formulated by the understanding. Thus, the understanding is assigned a position of high importance with respect to the reason. The understanding presents the reason with its concepts; reason is called upon to affirm or deny them. And, it is the responsibility of the understanding to formulate and interpret clearly its concepts. The "ideas" of reason are therefore judgments which have been made regarding the understanding's clearly interpreted concepts. And, the understanding must, therefore, be educated if the reason is to judge its concepts. Furthermore, the understanding must rely on impulses which are external or empirical; it cannot act of its own accord, but must act as a consequence of experience.

Outward matters give us the occasion which awakens consciousness, and spontaneous nature leads us to something higher than ourselves.

[The religious element] acts spontaneous and unconsciously, soon as the outward occasion offers.

[40] This difference has been carefully indicated in an article by George F. Newbrough on "Reason and Understanding in the Works of Theodore Parker," *The South Atlantic Quarterly* (January, 1948).
[41] *A Discourse of Religion*, p. 18.

When the occasion is given from without us. the reason, spontaneously, independent of our forethought and volition, acting by its own laws, gives us by intuition an idea.[42]

The intuition or reason is logically prior to experience; but because the intellect or the understanding or consciousness must be awakened by experience, the transcendental reason is empirically *a posteriori*. Thus, the initial duality in his method reflects Parker's theory of knowledge. The role played by the reason is not unlike the position ascribed to the deductive method; its judgments are universal principles. The intellect or understanding depends on "facts of observation" which are arrived at inductively, and are therefore particulars which are, through the action of reason, generalized. It was Parker's conclusion that the reason holds a place of final judgment, but that without the understanding, reason would be empty. Reason depends on the understanding; and, the understanding gains the final verdict for its concepts from reason. The implication of this theory of knowledge in the area of religion can be formulated as follows: the "instinctive intuition of the divine" is a judgment of reason, and depends for its "idea" of the divine on the educated, religious understanding. Thus, the "religious element" is comparable to the "intuition" or reason; but its expression depends on an awakening of the religious consciousness and, finally, on the educated views which the understanding formulates. The theory of knowledge which Parker outlined is, therefore, of central importance in his philosophy of religion.

Parker went on to state that the religious consciousness is initially awakened by man's "sense of dependence." Thus, his use of a modified Kantian emphasis was paralleled by his reference to Schleiermacher's interpretation of the basis of

42 *Ibid.*, pp. 6, 7–8, 9–10.

religion. The first of the "facts of man's religious consciousness [is] . . . a feeling of weakness." [43] The intuition, in
the area of religion, is initially confronted by "the consciousness of human finiteness"—*the* "idea" offered by the
intuition is "of that on which we depend." [44] Despite this
stress on the "sense of dependence," Parker did not follow
Schleiermacher completely; he did not use the word "absolute" before "dependence," though he did make use of
the unconditioned in his phrase, "absolute reverence, faith,
and love." By his failure to use Schleiermacher's whole
phrase, "absolute dependence," he evidently was avoiding
a traditional Lutheran or Calvinistic interpretation of the
basis of religion. But he was avoiding also an intensely subjective interpretation, which would make of religion merely
the expression of human feelings and desires; Feuerbach's
position seemed to Parker to be sheer atheism.[45]

But Parker did not hesitate to use the "sense of dependence" as the initial impetus which causes man to enter what
he spoke of as "the first stage of religious experience." The
emergence of self-awareness was, in general, conceived of
as the first indication of "religious consciousness." "As soon
as man has any personal self-consciousness, and feels 'I am
a me,' he has also a religious consciousness." [46] This initial
distinction between the individual and his environment was
interpreted as man's first motivation for investigating the
universe. The universe has two "hemispheres"; in "the

43 "The Facts of Religious Consciousness," pp. 234–235.
44 *A Discourse of Religion,* p. 10.
45 In a letter dated May 4, 1854 (quoted in Parker's *Works*), he said,
"There are some Germans who accept [Feuerbach] as their Coryphaeus
—atheistic men whose creed is: 'There is no God, Feuerbach is his
prophet; a body but no soul; a here, but no hereafter; a world and no
God."
46 "The Facts of Religious Consciousness," pp. 233–234.

world of matter" man is introduced to such particular facts
as motion, regularity, and various "signs of benevolence";
"the world of man" discloses the universal facts of love and
justice. But, in each case, according to this view, man becomes forcefully aware of his dependence on the universe;
he depends on it for his physical needs, and he depends on
it for his spiritual needs. Thus, dependence has two con-
notations, and man can rely on the universe about him, for
"we have perfect harmony in the relation between matter
and man." [47]

Man's "sense of dependence" has philosophical implications as well. Parker used this phrase in his argument for
belief in God; the "sense of dependence" was important to
him because it led directly to "that on which we depend."
This was his most concise interpretation of the correlation.
"A man forms a notion of his own existence. This notion
involves that of dependence, which conducts him back to
that on which dependence rests." [48] He nevertheless distinguished between the general and the more specific exercise
of the religious element with respect to dependence.

Our first spiritual act is the feeling of limitation, and so dependence, a general spiritual act. The first act of the religious
faculty is a feeling of somewhat that we depend on, a feeling of
God, a special act of the religious faculty.[49]

This was stated still more specifically when Parker iden-
tified dependence and finitude. The "argument by analogy"
which he formulated on the basis of this statement clearly
rests on only one assumption, the utter reliability of the

[47] "God in the Relation between Matter and Man," sermon iv of the
series on "God's Revelation in Matter and Mind"; *Works*, VI, 301.
[48] *A Discourse of Religion*, p. 145.
[49] "God in the World of Man," sermon iii of the series previously referred to; p. 273.

human faculties; to Parker this assumption was the primary condition for all rational thought.

Consciousness of the infinite is the condition of the consciousness of the finite. I learn of a finite thing by sensation, I get an idea thereof; at the same time the idea of the infinite unfolds in me. I am not conscious of my own existence except as a finite existence, that is, as a dependent existence; and the idea of the infinite, of God on whom I depend, comes at the same time as the logical correlative of a knowledge of myself. So the existence of God is a certainty.[50]

The existence of this religious element, our experience of this sense of dependence, this sentiment of something which bounds, is itself a proof by implication of the existence of its object. . . . A natural want in man's constitution implies satisfaction. . . . Thus the existence of God is implied by the natural sense of dependence; implied in the religious element itself; it is expressed by the spontaneous intuition of reason.[51]

The steps in this modified version of the classical cosmological argument are clearly stated: consciousness of finitude and dependence leads to a consciousness of the infinite; because the sense of dependence is natural in man, he may be sure that God, on whom he depends, exists. Briefly stated, Parker maintained, "I am; therefore God is." [52] Parker was, despite his frequent repetition of this view, aware of the dialectical limitations involved. He was familiar, he said, with Kant's demonstration of "the insufficiency of all the philosophical arguments for the existence of God." [53] Parker consequently made this theological doctrine ultimately a statement of belief. "The belief," he said, "always precedes the proof." [54] And, according to Parker, the be-

[50] "Transcendentalism," p. 33.   [51] *A Discourse of Religion*, pp. 9–10.
[52] "Transcendentalism," p. 33.   [53] *A Discourse of Religion*, p. 12.
[54] *Ibid.*, p. 12.

lief is a judgment of reason, which is given when the understanding has clearly presented to it the primary facts of
finitude and dependence.

The reconciliation of these loose interpretations of both
Kant and Schleiermacher formed what Parker called his
"spiritual philosophy," and may also be interpreted as his
version of "transcendentalism." It supplied a secure basis
for the belief that "religion is amenable to human nature."
"Truths of intuition" and "truths of demonstration" together formed the foundation of his "transcendentalism."
The "spontaneous" and the "voluntary" consciousness were
believed to be complementary. "The intuition of human nature" appeared to be the fundamental method of inquiry.
This method then offers evidence for the existence of a "religious element" and a "sense of dependence." These, in turn,
take the inquirer to the "certainty" of God's existence.
Thus, the "spiritual philosophy" provides, according to
Parker, an enduring foundation for Christianity; it lays a
basis for religious truth which is more permanent and enlightened than the external authorities set forth by orthodox Unitarians.

But in his statements regarding the "spiritual philosophy" it is apparent that Parker was equally anxious to
present a basis for spiritual truth which could protect
Christianity against the trend among transcendentalists to
transcend its essential doctrines. His own formulations had,
therefore, a double purpose: to withstand the perversions
of an uneducated dogmatism, and to weather the extreme
transcendentalist doctrine of self-reliance. His "transcendentalism" was consequently more critical than romantic.
It was more orderly and argumentative than epigrammatic

and oracular. It assigned a major role to the understanding, and refused to follow the views which subjected the understanding to the reason.

Because Parker interpreted his position in this way, it is necessary to distinguish clearly between his views and those which Emerson set forth in the *Divinity School Address*. It was not the gospel of individualistic self-reliance that Parker defended as he entered the controversy. When he referred to the truths of "intuition," he was speaking of universals or general principles, which have validity because they have received the sanction of reason, and because the understanding first clarified, then formulated, and finally presented justly its objective "concepts." Thus, intuitive truths are not "innate" truths ; nor are they particulars. It is true that his terminology, despite these attempts to clarify what he meant, was vague ; the fact that this may have been intentional is disconcerting. Noah Porter, Jr., who criticized Parker on theological grounds, was justified in attacking his "lack of clarity about the religious sentiment." [55]

But his fundamental confidence and purpose are unmistakable. Religion is based on human nature ; it expresses natural human ideals. It cannot be imposed from without, nor can its truths be proven through the use of references and authorities which are wholly external to man. Religion has its fundamental source in man's natural powers, and these powers can be examined by an analysis of the basic elements in human nature.

These affirmations of his "spiritual philosophy" were repeatedly contrasted with empiricism, or what he called "sen-

[55] Noah Porter, Jr., review of Parker's *Discourse of Religion* in the *New Englander,* vol. III (July, 1845), p. 50.

sationalism." His own position was clear: "man has faculties which transcend the senses; . . . the mind is a living principle which originates ideas *when the senses present the occasion.*" [56] This view ascribed an important place to the senses and to empirical knowledge. Parker believed that the mental scientists had

analyzed consciousness and by the inductive method established the conclusion that there is a consciousness that never was sensation, never could be; that our knowledge is *in part a priori;* that we know, 1, certain truths of necessity; 2, certain truths of intuition, or spontaneous consciousness; 3, certain truths of demonstration, a voluntary consciousness.[57]

This succinct statement of the basic view of transcendentalism was, however, not peculiar to Parker, for all transcendentalists placed emphasis on reason as the corrective to the empiricists' reliance on sensation. And, this interpretation of transcendentalism led Parker to expand the list of those whom he believed to be benefactors of the "new school of metaphysical philosophy." He included many divergent figures, since he believed that the German Biblical critics and critical historians had greatly aided the cause of transcendentalism. But Parker usually credited the development of the "spiritual philosophy" to the traditional figures. He was, nevertheless, critical as he surveyed their contributions. He spoke of Wordsworth, Carlyle, and Coleridge.

The writings of Wordsworth were becoming familiar to the thoughtful lovers of nature and of man, and drawing men to natural piety. Carlyle's works got reprinted at Boston, diffusing a strong, and then, also, a healthy influence on old and young. The writings of Coleridge were reprinted in America, all of them "Aids to Reflection," and brilliant with scattered sparks

[56] "Transcendentalism," p. 23.   [57] *Ibid.*

of genius; they incited many to think, more especially young trinitarian ministers; and, spite of the lack of both historic and philosophic accuracy, and the utter absence of all proportion in his writing, spite of his haste, his vanity, prejudice, sophistry, confusion, and opium—yet he did a great service to New England.[58]

The French group of "Eclectic philosophers" were also included, with special mention of the genius of Victor Cousin's "brilliant Mosaic." Cousin had "helped to free the young men from gross sensationalism . . . and the grosser supernaturalism of the ecclesiastical theology"; [59] he had "popularized the discoveries of psychology, which furnishes a magazine whence theological supplies may be drawn." [60] But Parker viewed with suspicion Cousin's numerous "errors, his hasty generalizations, and presumptuous flights." [61]

Such a seventeenth century "spiritual thinker" as Ralph Cudworth was also on Parker's list of the benefactors of transcendentalism; Cudworth's *True Intellectual System* was a "stupendous pile of learning." [62] Early in his career Parker had considered editing and republishing this classic of Cambridge Platonism.[63] He was attracted by Cudworth's erudition and particularly by his vindication of a theistic faith on the basis of "revelations" and the psychology of the spiritual faculties. He was nevertheless critical of Cudworth on several counts: his thoughts were seldom ex-

---

[58] "Experience as a Minister," pp. 309–310.   [59] *Ibid.*, p. 310.
[60] "Thoughts on Theology," pp. 158–159.   [61] *Ibid.*, p. 159.
[62] "Cudworth's Intellectual System," *The Christian Examiner*, Vol. XXVII (January, 1840); *Works*, Vol. XIV.
[63] This task was obviated by Harrison's edition, which included the notes Mosheim had added to the original work; this edition appeared in 1845; it was Mosheim's edition which had been used earlier to introduce Cudworth's System to the Continent, a task which was successfully carried out by Le Clerc.

pressed in a clear and orderly arrangement; his long paragraphs were loaded with many antiquarianisms and irrelevancies; his historical and critical judgments were often completely in error; and he repeatedly showed a deference to authorities who were actually of no decisive importance, or he maintained opinions which varied directly with the best information available.

Despite the limitations detected in all these works, Parker included the authors among those who had encouraged the rise in America of a "transcendentalist" or "spiritual" philosophy. The emphasis made by them he contrasted with the views of such sensationalists as "Bacon, Hobbes, Locke, Paley, and Hume . . . the greatest thinkers of this tribe." [64] Parker interpreted sensationalism or "naturalism" as the doctrine that

there is nothing in the intellect which was not first in the senses. Here "intellect" means the whole . . . consciousness of man. . . . The senses afford a sensation. I reflect upon this, and by reflection transform a sensation into an idea. An idea therefore is a transformed sensation.[65]

He did not criticize sensationalism for its emphasis on sense data, but rejected the belief that the "ideas" of reason are nothing more than "transformed sensations." Sensationalism distorted the essential purpose of scientific inquiry. As has been noted with reference to his stress on the understanding, Parker had great faith in the scientific method. He said that he had respect for "the power of science; [it] depends not only on the mind itself, but on the nice relation between that and the world of matter outside." [66] And,

[64] "Theological and Philosophical Development in New England," *Works*, VI, 353.   [65] "Transcendentalism," p. 7.
[66] "The World of Matter and the Spirit of Man," sermon v in the series referred to above (*op. cit.*, p. 319).

Parker praised the encouragement empiricism had given to scientific inquiry. In America it was Benjamin Franklin who, according to Parker, had begun natural scientific investigations primarily because of the stimulation he had received from Francis Bacon. But Parker was critical of the empiricists for their failure to go beyond investigation to the establishment of universal principles and general laws. They had elaborated "no idea of cause, except that of empirical connection in time and place; no idea of substance, only of body, or form of substance; no ontology, but phenomenology." [67] Because empiricism had not ventured beyond a strict reliance on sense data, Parker attacked it as a system which was wholly materialistic and mechanistic. Phenomenological conclusions in the physical realm it carried over into the fields of politics, ethics, and religion; its political dictum was "might makes right," but it failed to make any distinction between the might, as well as the right, of a monarchy, an oligarchy, or a democracy. Its ethics could be reduced to the term "expediency," since all decisions were based only on the utilitarian principle. To religion, sensationalism had contributed only a foundation for the distortions of orthodoxy. "This system of naturalism is the philosophy which lies at the foundation of the popular theology of New England." [68] Its fundamental hypothesis was that of an imperfect and finite God, whose relationship to the universe was based on miracles. Consequently, all of its other doctrines were distortions.

This theory reduces the idea of God to that of an abstract cause . . . It reduces the soul to the aggregate functions of the flesh; providence to a law of matter; infinity to a dream; religion

[67] "Transcendentalism," p. 9.   [68] *A Discourse of Religion*, p. 181.

to priestcraft; prayer to an apostrophe; morality to making a good bargain; conscience to cunning.[69]

These distortions, basic to sensationalism and taken over by orthodoxy, were referred to by Parker as "the 'original sin' of the Anglo-Saxon people." [70] In the closing years of his life he was convinced that "a more spiritual philosophy has begun to take the place of the sensational, one not founded at all on the traditional claims of miraculous revelation, but on the spiritual nature of man himself." [71]

There is still another reason for Parker's allegiance to the spiritual philosophy of transcendentalism. He believed that it related the functioning of the four basic elements in human nature and thus revealed the universal "intuitions" of man. He seldom spoke of the religious element without relating it to the other "spiritual faculties"—the intellectual, the affectional, and the moral judgments of reason. His doctrine of "manliness" was Parker's characteristic formulation of the harmonious interrelationship of these elements. By "manliness" he meant "the four forms of piety."

Piety of mind, the love of truth, is only a fragment of piety; piety of conscience, the love of right, is also fragmentary; so is love of men, piety of the heart. . . . We want to unite them all with the consciousness of God, into a complete, perfect, and total religion. . . . Consider the power of religion in a man whose mind and conscience. heart, and soul, are well developed. He has these four forms of piety; they all unite, each to all and all to each.[72]

[69] *Ibid.*, p. 179.
[70] "Theological and Philosophical Development in New England," p. 353.
[71] "Theological and Philosophical Development in New England," I, 364.
[72] "Of Conscious Religion and the Soul," *Works*, III, 125, 130.

It is already clear from our discussion of the role of the understanding what Parker meant by the intellectual faculty. The affectional element in human nature is a factor man discovers in his own hemisphere of the universe; it is man's natural inclination to love God and his fellow men. The moral faculty must be examined in somewhat greater detail. Parker believed that man has an inherent and natural basis for distinguishing between right and wrong, good and evil, freedom and slavery, justice and tyranny. This natural power is, therefore, a "fact of consciousness"; it is the spontaneous awareness of moral law. Parker spoke of this power as the conscience—"that eternal law of right God wrote in us for our rule of conduct, personal and social." [73] "The conscience of each man is to him the moral standard; so to mankind is the conscience of the race. In morals conscience is complete and reliable." [74] Thus, Parker could outline the method he followed in social and moral reform.

I endeavored to establish philosophically the moral principle I should appeal to, and show its origin in the constitution of man, to lay down the natural law so plain that all might acknowledge and accept it; next I attempted to show what welfare had followed in human history from keeping this law, and what misery from violating it; then I applied this moral principle of nature and the actual experience of history to the special public vice I wished to whelm over. Such a process may seem slow; I think it is the only one sure of permanent good effects.[75]

Parker referred here to "justice" as the moral principle; it is a universal judgment of reason, and it is therefore the ultimate verdict in the field of morals. "Love of justice," he said, "is the moral part of piety." [76] Religion must also be

[73] "Man in His Religious Aspects," *ibid.*, V, 333.
[74] "Transcendentalism," p. 29.   [75] "Experience as a Minister," p. 362.
[76] "Of Justice and the Conscience," *Works*, III, 57.

defined in its relation to "moral piety"—morality is the external "hemisphere" of piety whereas the love of God is within man's heart. "The love of man" is, therefore, the correlative of "the absolute love of God."

> Religion is voluntary obedience to the law of God, *inward and outward obedience,* to that law he has written on our nature. . . .

> The highest notion I can form of religion is this: . . . conscious service of the infinite God by keeping every law he has enacted into the constitution of the universe,—service of him by the normal use, discipline, development, and delight of every limb of the body, every faculty of the spirit, and so of all the powers we possess.[77]

It has been previously noted that Parker, like Kant, preached a gospel of reconciliation between faith and reason. He also followed Kant in the belief that religion must express itself in "practical holiness." Nevertheless, he was cautious in identifying religion with morality and criticized Kant for having isolated a system of morals unrelated to religion.

> Now there are two tendencies connected with religion, one is speculative; here the man is intellectually employed in matters pertaining to religion, to God, to man's religious nature, and his relation and connection with God. The result of this tendency is theology. This is not religion itself. . . . The other is practical; here the man is employed in acts of obedience to religion. The result of this tendency is morality. This alone is not religion itself, but one part of the life religion demands. . . . A sharp analysis separates between the religious and moral elements in a man.[78]

Here is an implicit criticism of the Kantian extreme. Another statement sharpens the criticism with respect to Christology:

[77] *A Discourse of Religion,* pp. 33, 35.   [78] *Ibid.,* pp. 34–36.

[His] system has excellences and defects. By exalting the idea of moral goodness, Kant led men to acknowledge an absolute spiritual power, showing that this is the common ground between philosophy and Christianity, and with this begins the reconciliation of the two.[79] He recognized the divine as something dwelling in man, and therefore filled up the chasm, as it were, between the two natures. Again, he acknowledged no authority so long as it was merely outward and not legitimated in the soul, for he had felt the slavery incident upon making the historical a dogma. He saw the mind cannot be bound by anything merely external, for that has value only so far as it contains the idea and makes it historical. But, on the other hand, *he exalts the subjective too high, and does not legitimate the internal moral law.* . . . His foundation therefore is unstable until this is done. Besides he is not consistent with himself; for while he ascribes absolute power to this innate ideal of a perfect man, he leaves nothing for the historical appearance of the God-man. He makes his statutory form useless, if not injurious, and makes a dualistic antithesis between reason and God. Still more is it inconsistent with Christianity; for it *makes morality the whole of religion;* it cuts off all connection between the divine and human life by denying that influence comes down from God upon man.[80]

Basing his argument on Christian theology, the nature of "inspiration," and Biblical scholarship, Parker alleges that Kant set forth a purely secular system of ethics on the weak foundation of "the subjective" and that he thereby denied the distinctive aspects of Christianity. Parker's own position is clear: He underscored the moral aspect of religion as its external aspect. It is therefore related but not identical with religion.

Parker did not develop a "moral theology" and he did not theologize moral problems. In his "doctrine of manli-

[79] Parker believed that Leibniz had attempted to affect this.
[80] "Thoughts on Theology," pp. 205–206.

ness" he stressed the harmonious interrelationship of all of the spiritual faculties, stressing both the subjective and the objective parts of piety:

We need . . . religion for its general and its special purposes; need it as subjective piety in each of these fragmentary forms, as joined into a totality of religious consciousness; we need it as morality, keeping the natural laws of God for the body and the spirit, in the individual, domestic, social, national, and general human or cosmic form, the divine sentiment becoming the human act. We need this to heal the vices of modern society, to revolutionize this modern feudalism of gold, and join the rich and poor, the employer and the employed, in one bond of human fellowship; we need it to break down the wall between class and class, nation and nation, race and race—to join all classes into one nation, all nations into one great human family. Science alone is not adequate to achieve this; calculations of interest cannot affect it; political economy will not check the iron hand of power, nor relax the grasp of the oppressor from his victim's throat. Only religion, deep, wide-spread, and true, can achieve this work.[81]

A life obedient to the love of God and of man—that is the sacramental form of religion. All else is means, provisional; this the end, a finality.[82]

Someday there will be churches built in which it shall be taught that the only outward service God asks is goodness, and truth is the only creed; that a divine life—piety in the heart, morality in the hand—is the only real worship. Men will use symbols or not, as they like . . . Worship will be fresh and natural . . . Truth for the creed, goodness for the form, love for the baptism.[83]

To Parker, "manly religion" is "the natural and real ordinance of religion." Manliness is achieved when the four fac-

[81] "Of Conscious Religion and the Soul," p. 138.
[82] "Of Conventional and Natural Sacraments," the *Works of Theology*, III, 255.
[83] "The Excellence of Goodness," *ibid.*, IV, 228–229.

ulties cooperate harmoniously in the development of a fourfold piety. Society can be revolutionized by such manliness;
and the Church, with its natural foundations, can be transformed. For religion is more than morality: it is worship,
piety, morality, love, goodness, and truth. It ascends to its
highest position when in the individual, or in society, the
powers of human nature—intellectual, affectional, moral,
and religious—work together toward the achievement of an
ultimate goal: the full acceptance and understanding of
truth, pure and disinterested love, perfect obedience to the
love of God and man, and the full worship of the heart.

"Manliness" also carried another meaning as used by
Parker: it expressed what he meant by "self-esteem" and in
this connotation was of extreme personal importance to
him. When he felt isolated by those who condemned his
radical views and who criticized him for his reform work,
Parker was called upon to practice the "self-esteem" involved in being manly.

I feel it is not altogether pleasant to stand alone, to be viewed
with suspicion and hatred. Blessed are those men who can take
things as they find them, believe as the mob believes, and sail on
the wave of public opinion. I remember you said a year ago, he
that defies public opinion, like the man who spits into the wind,
spits in his own face. It is so. But what then? Let it be so. Better
men have found less sympathy than I.[84]

Soon I found that I was not welcome to the American market,
state, church, nor press. It could not be otherwise; yet I confess
I had not anticipated so thorough a separation. . . .

I knew at the beginning what I must expect; that at first men
younger than I, who had not learned over much, would taunt
me with my youth; that others, not scholarly, would charge me
with lack of learning competent for my task; and cautious old

[84] Letter to Dr. Francis, February 14, 1842; this letter is in the possession of the Boston Public Library.

men, who did not find it convenient to deny my facts, or answer my arguments, would cry out, "This young man must be put down!" and set their venerable popular feet in that direction. . . .

It will not always be unpopular justly to seek the welfare of all men.[85]

With such views, you see in what esteem I must be held by society, church, and state. I cannot be otherwise than hated. This is the necessity of my position—that I must be hated. . . .

How could it be otherwise? Men who knew no God but a jealous God, no human nature but total depravity, no religion but the ordinances of baptism, the Lord's Supper, and reverence for ancient words of holy men, and the like; no truth but public opinion, no justice but public law, no earthly good above respectability—they must needs hate me, and I do not wonder at it.[86]

He often seemed to welcome and to exaggerate the hatred of those who held him in low esteem; he called them "modern Pharisees."

But while these . . . Pharisees pursue their wicked way, the path of real manliness . . . opens before each soul of us all. The noblest sons of God have trodden therein, so that no one need wander. Moses, and Jesus, and John, and Paul have gained their salvation by being real men; content to see goodness and God, they found their reward; they blessed the nations of the earth, and entered the kingdom of religious souls.[87]

So, the ultimate reward of manliness is "salvation," and "being a real man" is to join the universal company of "seers" of universal truth. Here lay the source of Parker's confidence and his courage.

[85] "Experience as a Minister," pp. 342–348, 388, 411.
[86] "Some Account of My Ministry," a sermon in two parts, preached on November 14 and 21, 1852; *Works*, XIII, 64–65, 72.
[87] "The Pharisees," a sermon preached on January 24, 1841; it was reprinted in *The Dial* (July, 1841); *Works*, IV, 125.

The "spiritual philosophy" which Parker outlined stressed, therefore, the universal truths of our common human nature. He believed that religion and morality, knowledge and love, have their *objective* basis in human nature. He emphasized also his belief that as the fullest human life is the result of a harmonious relationship between the four fundamental or universal elements in human nature, so absolute religion is permanent and universal, because it unites the universal truths, affections, justice, and manly piety. Emerson, on the contrary, in his address at the Divinity School in 1838, appealed to each individual soul to trust its own "authentic" revelations. For him truths or principles revealed in the soul are intensely personal. This is, therefore, the basic contrast, not contradiction, between Parker's views and Emerson's *Divinity School Address:* Parker underscored the universal and permanent elements of human consciousness and experience, while Emerson stressed the "authenticity" of the individual soul and its personal, fresh insights. Thus, in the *Levi Blodgett Letter* and in his other contributions to the controversy, Parker was not merely defending Emerson's position as it was outlined by him in the Address of 1838. Emerson, too, had a tendency to look for "the miraculous in the common." Thus, against both Norton and Emerson, Parker defended his confidence in the unity of reason and understanding; he also stressed the importance of evidence over inspiration. The doctrine of the relation between the "reason" and the "understanding" was an important issue between Emerson and Parker. While Emerson followed the general Coleridgian emphasis on the reason at the expense of the understanding, Parker clearly stressed the significant part played by the understanding in the gaining of rational knowledge.

Again, at first glance, Parker's doctrine of "self-esteem" appears to be a modified restatement of Emerson's doctrine of self-reliance. But, Parker's emphasis in this respect is fundamentally objective, while Emerson's is subjective. For Parker "self-esteem" was not identical with self-confidence based on the possession of individual "insights"; rather it was a participation in the universal community for which universal truths are both absolute and enduring. These several contrasts are essentially one: Parker's emphasis on the *permanent* as opposed to Emerson's stress on the *personal*, or Parker's interest in *universal intuitions* or *principles*, as opposed to Emerson's interest in the *individual consciousness* and its truths.

Thus far, our consideration of Parker's "spiritual philosophy" has dealt primarily with his examination of human nature in order to determine its four interrelated elements and the piety which expresses "total" religion. But we have examined only one half of the methodology which he set forth; we have limited ourselves to the arguments which he based on "the intuition of human nature" and "the primitive facts of consciousness." We must now show how Parker combined this deductive aspect of his twofold method with an interest in "proving" the facts thus arrived at by the experimental and observational study of human history. It should be clear to us that Parker did not look to the reason for "proofs"; the reason does not "prove" truths of the understanding, but it "legitimates" them; through its judgment, the truths are given additional "sanction." Proof must, on the other hand, be based on the empirical method; thus, the study of human history is valid as a method of "proving" the universals which reason has already sanctioned.

Transcendentalism, according to Parker, discovers through an analysis of human nature the universal or permanent bases of religion and morality. By deductive analysis it arrives at precisely the same objective truths that can be discovered inductively either by Biblical or historical criticism. And, as the inductive understanding must present its concepts to the reason for final judgment, so must the "facts of consciousness" be substantiated as "facts of observation." These are among the reasons Parker gave for his extensive study of history.

He believed in the progressive development and growth of the human faculties and concluded that "the idea of progress" is the central fact revealed by historical study. While he did not construct an original philosophy of history, his erudition became his most important tool for the theory of progress. He criticized the historian who is merely an annalist, since his responsibility is to interpret and evaluate his data. The true historian is a biographer. Of William H. Prescott's writings on the domestic and colonial history of Spain Parker wrote:

he tells the facts for the facts' sake. Hence there are no pages in the book, perhaps no sentences, which the reader turns back to read a second time, to see if the thought be true; here are the facts of history without the thought which belongs to the facts.[88]

We have a right to insist that [the historian] shall give us the philosophy of history, and report the lessons thereof, as well as record the facts.[89]

Because history has an "organic" continuity, a plan, or a purpose, all historical writers should attempt to determine what its meaning is. From this belief, Parker was led

[88] "Prescott as an Historian," *The Massachusetts Quarterly Review*, No. 6 (March, 1849); *Works*, VIII, 218.   [89] *Ibid.*, p. 183.

to study the history of various religions in order to substantiate the hypothesis that religious experience is universal and that it moves progressively from a crude stage
of fetichistic primitivism toward an enlightened monotheism
which, in the end, becomes the "absolute" religion. He was
further led to study general history as the social scientist
and the moralist study human experience.

Believing that historical data have meaning only when
viewed within the context of a cultural or "organic" pattern, Parker was greatly interested in the type of "people's
biography" that George Bancroft was making popular.[90]
He praised historians who combined their critical and analytical judgment with high ethical standards, and who recorded the intellectual endeavors of a people along with the
events of their times. The historian was urged to prepare
himself

to tell what ought to be, for he is to pass judgment on events,
and try counsels by their causes first and their consequences not
less. When all these things are told, history ceases to be a mere
panorama of events having no unity, but time and place; it becomes philosophy teaching by experience, and has a profound
meaning and awakens a deep interest, while it tells the lessons
of the past for the warning of the present and the edification of
the future.[91]

Parker's ideal for history is summed up in the phrase, "it
becomes philosophy teaching by experience." The basic
lesson man can learn through his study of experience in
history is the fact of progressive development; "man advances continually." [92] This is the fundamental meaning

[90] Bancroft's *History of the United States* (3 vols., Boston, 1834–40),
with its stress on "the American people," was one of the works on history that Parker appreciated most.
[91] "Prescott as an Historian," p. 178.
[92] "Human Progress"; *Works*, V, 287.

and significance in history; this gives it its continuity and
its purpose. And, according to Parker, the advance proceeds through a series of given stages. In a paragraph dealing primarily with his disillusionment regarding reform
activity, he labels three:

> I knew there were three periods in each great movement of man-
> kind—that of *sentiment, ideas,* and *action.* I fondly hoped the
> last had come; but when I found I had reckoned without the
> host, I turned my attention to the two former, and sought to
> arouse the sentiment of justice and mercy, and to diffuse the
> ideas which belong to . . . reformation.[93]

The view that progress takes place according to three stages
of scientific development was known to Parker as Auguste
Comte's general theory of progress. But Parker does not
conform to Comte's view that moral, intellectual, and political development proceeds through the "theological" and
the "metaphysical" stages in order finally to enter the
"positivistic stage of historical experience." [94] While he
may have been influenced by Comte, his position was more
nearly derived from the work of Henry Thomas Buckle.
From its first appearance, Parker was deeply interested in
Buckle's *History of Civilization in England.* To Professor
Henry D. Rogers in Edinburgh, he wrote in December,
1857:

> I think it is a great book, and know none so important since the
> *Novum Organum* of Bacon. I mean none in English. Of course
> I except the *Principia* of Newton. This is a *Novum Organum*
> in the department of history—the study of man; it is a *restau-
> ratio maxima.* Nobody here ever heard the name of Henry
> Thomas Buckle before. If you can tell me, I wish you would;

93 "Experience as a Minister," p. 345.
94 The full statement of Comte's view is elaborated in his major work
on the *System of Positive Philosophy* (published in six volumes at
intervals between 1830 and 1842).

and also what is thought of the book in that northern Athens where you dwell. In many particulars it reminds me of *The Vestiges of the Natural History of Creation*. I don't always agree with the author . . . but always think him a great man. His learning also is admirable.[95]

Parker admired Buckle's erudition and believed him to be eminently qualified for his great task. He was also keenly interested in Buckle's tendency to attach extreme importance to geographical and environmental factors in the development of a culture. He was attracted also by Buckle's portrayal of the development in the physical and natural sciences, and by the generalization that all the fields of man's endeavors are developing toward independent and critical sciences. Thus, Buckle's "scientific view of history" was compatible with Parker's own. On it Parker relied heavily in a series of sermons on "God's Revelation in Matter and Mind" of which he repeatedly spoke as the culmination of his sermonic writings. Buckle's interpretation of religion—that, looking on history generally, the religions of mankind are effects of man's improvement and not the cause of progress [96]—Parker considered an important contribution to the comparative study of culture and religion.

Of greatest importance was Buckle's basic thesis that a role of major significance must be assigned to man's "ideas of social progress." John Stuart Mill and Buckle were in fundamental agreement in their conclusion that the increase of knowledge is the primary force behind the human advance. This view had, of course, been stated often. It is as ancient as Greek philosophy. In modern thought, Francis

[95] A letter to Professor Henry D. Rogers, Edinburgh, December 29, 1857; see John Weiss, *The Life and Correspondence of Theodore Parker,* I, 334.
[96] See his *History of Civilization in England,* Chaps. V–VI.

Bacon and Condorcet made it the basis of their views. Hegel's explanation of history emphasized the career of human reason as the continuity of historical evolution. Lessing made use of a similar interpretation in order to state a divine plan for the education of the human race. But, Buckle explained the intellectualistic interpretation of progress most elaborately. He believed that ideas have historical power, and that society must continually assure itself of having the resources of knowledge at hand if it is to progress intellectually. He furthermore combined a moral conditioning factor with the intellectual. And, he believed that the two fold test of civilization is moral and intellectual elevation. But his primary emphasis was upon the intellectual element: it is more progressive and more permanent in its results; and intellectual gains are more easily collected, preserved, and transmitted. This is, therefore, his general conclusion: according to a comprehensive view of civilization, changes occur, first, because of the knowledge possessed by the ablest men of the society; secondly, because that knowledge is directed toward the elevation of the society; and, thirdly, and above all, because the knowledge is diffused and spread freely through all of the classes of the society.

This conclusion is reflected in Parker's statement of his own position regarding historical development. As we have seen, he believed that such development proceeds through three distinct stages—sentiments, ideas, and action. He also believed that the law of progress is illustrated repeatedly. It is illustrated in the development of the elements in human nature, and the fourfold form of piety basic to the doctrine of manliness is the highest culmination of this aspect of progressive development. Evolutionary development is, according to Parker, particularly notable in the progress of religion in history.

His intensive study of the history of religions had a two-fold purpose. He attempted to show, first, that all men, throughout all of human history and in every civilization, offer empirical evidence for the existence of the religious element. He endeavored, secondly, to distinguish between the numerous and varied transient elements of religions and the permanent or universal elements. This distinction which could be determined on the basis of his fundamental methodology, indicated the measure to which a given religion has attained an approximation of the ideal, the universal, or the "absolute." In religion as in all other phases of human activity there is demonstrated a genuine evolutionary development. Of his researches Parker wrote:

I studied the historical development of religion and theology amongst the nations . . . Jewish, and Christian, . . . the Brahmanic, the Buddhistic, the Classic, and the Mohammetan. As far as possible, . . . I studied the sacred books of mankind in their original tongues, and with the help of the most faithful interpreters. . . . I attended pretty carefully to the religions of savages and barbarians. . . . I found no tribe of men destitute of religion who had attained power of articulate speech.[97]

The phenomena of religion—like those of science and art—must vary from land to land, and age to age, with the varying civilization of mankind. . . . Religious history is the tale of confusion. But looking deeper, we see it as a series of developments, all tending towards one great and beautiful end. . . . It leads through active obedience to an absolute trust, a perfect love; to the complete harmony of the finite man with the infinite God.[98]

[97] "Experience as a Minister," p. 300.
[98] *A Discourse of Religion*, pp. 38, 93–94, 129.

From the beginning of human history . . . there has been a progress in the visible results of this development of the religious faculties. The progress appears in the rise, decline, and disappearance of various forms of religion . . . In each case the form of religion . . . represented the highest development of the religious faculties of those people at that time, . . . [but] men must necessarily outgrow any specific and imperfect form of religion, . . . just as they outgrow each specific and imperfect form of science. Human nature continually transcends the facts of human history.[99]

These statements are suggestive of several aspects of Parker's historical study of religion which are worthy of careful consideration. Here, as in his ideas regarding the stages of general historical development, Parker outlined the categories or stages according to which religious development might be interpreted. Early in his career he attempted to establish the "classifications" of religion:

What do you think a good classification of religions? I would rather say *forms of worship,* since there is but one religion. That into *Polytheistic* and *Monotheistic* is mainly cutaneous. Is it not better to arrange them from their starting point, whether they take a *finite letter, book,* or *creed,* as the Jewish, Mohammedan, and the religion of the Christian church, both Protestant and Catholic, or take *the soul*—i.e., *God in man*—as the old Greeks and Jesus did? In one case, there results a *system,* hard as a pebble; in the other a method, capable of infinite applications. Is this a sound principle of arrangement? [100]

But this proposed method was, apparently, too limited and too subjective for his purpose. In his later writings, he names three basic stages or categories and two transitional phases; fetichism, polytheism, and monotheism were the

[99] *Theism, Atheism, and the Popular Theology,* a volume of sermons first published in 1853, pp. 124–125.
[100] Letter to Dr. Francis, February 14, 1840; in the possession of the Boston Public Library.

first three, and the remaining two were pantheism and dualism. To Parker, fetichism is "the infancy of religion," [101] the stage of miracles or magic, the "primitive" level of religious experience. As it develops beyond the lowest and most crude level, fetichism becomes synonymous with what is usually described as animism; "all the mass of created things [are] fetiches, . . . [and God is] not considered as distinct from the universe." [102] Pantheism, the first transitional stage, Parker characterized as the presence of a more conscious association of God with "created things"; it is therefore a refinement of fetichism. Polytheism was described as the stage in which several or many "impersonal powers" are distinguished from one another.

Polytheism clarifies the distinction between "material" and "spiritual" nature. Nevertheless, it describes God anthropomorphically. Several other characteristics of polytheism were outlined by Parker; it is the stage during which a distinct priesthood emerges; war is the normal state in polytheistic society, since it creates civil hostilities; slavery, one of the results of this warfare, is condoned by the priests and condemned by the prophets; the standard of morality may, nevertheless, be extremely high.[103]

Dualism, the second transitional stage, was described as "the deification of two principles, the absolute good, and the greatest evil." [104] Parker believed that Zoroastrianism best illustrated the continuing historical form of dualism. When dualism's fundamental contradiction is resolved—that is, when the negative and positive principles are made subject to one God—the stage of monotheism is achieved. Most important among the traits listed by Parker as characteristic

---

[101] *A Discourse of Religion,* p. 42. [102] *Ibid.*
[103] See *ibid.,* pp. 51–74. [104] *Ibid.,* p. 74.

of monotheism are the following: Numerous distinctions
between men on the basis of race, class, or nation are erased,
at least theoretically, since the one God is equally the Father
of all. Its doctrine of universal inspiration makes irrelevant
the artificial distinctions made, in earlier stages, between
the sacred and profane, the priestly and the secular. Because the God of monotheistic religion is conceived of as
transcendent, its theology is intentionally vague, and its
descriptions of God are attempts at avoiding anthropo-
morphic limitations. While it seeks to make clear the demand of obedience to moral law, this obedience is eventually
superseded by the concept of universal love. In its highest
development, slavery and war are outlawed. Though its
criteria are not always absolute, monotheism distinguishes
always between "truth" and "error." Finally, this stage of
religion, because of its accumulated historical dynamic,
prepares the way for further and more accelerated reform
and development.

The religions cited as monotheistic were Judaism, Mo-
hammedanism, and Christianity. Of these, "essential Christianity"—"the mode of religion [Jesus] taught, its sublime faith in God, its profound humanity" [105]—represented
the highest development. Parker spoke of it as "the ideal
of religion," "religion without limitations," or the "absolute religion." Absolute or "natural" religion was conceived
of as the culmination of the free expression of the universal
religious element. It is an "ideal" which Parker thought
possible within history; absolute religion is, according to
his view, the religion which belongs to the highest development of history. He therefore used this view of the ideal of
religion as the actual criterion of what religion should be;

[105] *Ibid.*, p. 232.

he used his view for typical prophetic purposes. With it he distinguished between "the transient and the permanent," the vestiges of primitive or "miraculous" stages of religious development, and the enlightened or "rational" dogmas of absolute religion. He came to the controversy in 1840 with his major weapon; he was armed with an absolute which he had "derived from the real revelation of God—this outward universe of matter, this inward universe of man." [106] And, having proved the validity of his "revelation" by the analytical study of human history, he used his "absolute," like a Hebrew prophet, to destroy the dogmatism of those who had only "a verbal revelation of God." It was to his absolute religion that he referred when he said, "the religion I preach will be the religion of enlightened men for the next thousand years." [107]

This survey of Parker's interest in historical criticism underscores the second aspect of his twofold methodology as he related the essential basis of religion to human nature and to human experience in history. He appealed both to "facts of consciousness" and to the "lessons of history." Each of these are sets of facts which illustrate and validate the universality and the permanence of "essential" Christianity as the historical religion which approximates the "absolute." As it is significant that Parker interpreted the "facts of consciousness" as the universal facts of mankind's consciousness, so too it is significant that he had a philosophy of history, for it is the history of mankind that offers "proof" for the universal principles of consciousness.

There is, nevertheless, a fundamental difference between these two sets of "facts": the analysis of consciousness dis-

[106] *Theism, Atheism, and the Popular Theology*, p. 231.
[107] *Ibid.*, p. 1.

closes a priori universals, while the study of history begins
with particulars in order to arrive at universals. Historical
study, therefore, sets out with the aim of collecting manifold data in order that it may formulate the universal principles or "lessons" which can be derived from the numerous
facts; this gives importance to "the *scientific* view of history." The analysis of human nature, on the other hand,
offers evidence for the four elements of man's nature, which,
in turn, through reason elaborate the four corrolary aspects of "manliness" as universal axioms; the universal
axioms must then be demonstrated objectively by the study
of history, so that they will be scientifically acceptable
"lessons."

Once again, the contrast between Emerson's emphasis on
individual inspiration, as stated in his *Divinity School
Address*, and Parker's emphasis on the permanent universals of human history and consciousness is unmistakable.
Emerson's individualistic appeal is foreign to Parker's
"spiritual philosophy," and Parker's intensive examination
of human experience in history is foreign to Emerson's
transcendentalism. Emerson, because his "revelations" are
essentially personal, would see only incidental value in the
corroboration which "facts of history" give to present, individual meaning. Parker, on the contrary, believed that
the historical validation of universals is the task which historical scholars should consider primary. The historian has,
according to Parker, the responsibility of demonstrating,
on the basis of particular data, that religion, as well as
truth, justice, and love, is "amenable to human nature."

Chapter 4

THE THEOLOGY OF ABSOLUTE
RELIGION

Parker's aim of developing a theology adequate to history's highest representation of religion was actually the culmination of his career. Before we can fully understand his theological views, it is necessary to examine his criticism of the "popular" theology. His "design" was

to recall men from the transient form to the eternal substance; from outward and false belief to real and inward life; from this partial theology and its idols of human device, to that universal religion and its ever-living infinite God; from the temples of human folly and sin, which every day crumble and fall, to the inner sanctuary of the heart where the still small voice will never cease to speak. I would show men religion as she is—most fair of all God's fairest children.[1]

The clear statement of what he meant by the theology which is outward, false, and partial was, therefore, the important preliminary step in his theological investigations. He thought of the "popular" theology as the greatest obstacle to the development of perfect or absolute religion. When he associated it with the orthodox Unitarians, he called it the "ecclesiastical theology"; when his context was Biblical criticism, he called it the "gloomy doctrine of infallible revelation." What he really meant can best be expressed by referring to the dogmas distinctive of sectarian or ecclesi-

[1] "Introduction," *A Discourse of Religion,* pp. xx–xxi.

astical orthodoxy. He explained that while Calvinism had
been initially set forth as a philosophical system, it had
degenerated into a narrow system of "partial" dogmas,
while Catholicism had degenerated into an equally distort-
ing veneration of the Church and ecclesiastical tradition.
Parker's summary of the doctrinal structure of the popular
theology is succinct:

There are five doctrines common to [this] theology, namely—
the false idea of God, as imperfect in power, wisdom, justice,
benevolence, and holiness; the false idea of man, as fallen, depraved, and by nature lost; the false idea of the relation between God and man, a relation of perpetual antagonism, man
naturally hating God, and God hating "fallen" and "depraved"
man; the false idea of inspiration, that it comes only by a miracle on God's part, not by normal action on man's; and the false
idea of salvation, that it is from the "wrath of God," who is "a
consuming fire" breaking out against "poor human nature," by
the "atoning blood of Christ," that is by the death of Jesus of
Nazareth, which appeased the "wrath of God," and on condition of belief in this popular theology, especially of the five
false ideas.[2]

Parker made two basic criticisms of this theology. He believed, first, that it is uneducated, unenlightened, and obviously false. He thought that "all the weapons of science"
should, therefore, be turned against it. This criticism was
often stated in a subtle manner. He asked, Who can believe
its doctrines? Certainly men of learning and men of science
cannot. The popular theology is a system unworthy of edu-

[2] "The Function of the Teacher of Religion," a sermon preached at the
ordination of Marshall Gunnison Kemball (his first "ordination sermon" after the South Boston Sermon), June 13, 1855; Parker's *Works,*
IV, 303–304. This summary was elaborated more fully in his *Sermons
of Theism, Atheism, and the Popular Theology,* pp. 124–191; it was
reiterated also in "A Discourse of the Relation between the Ecclesiastical Institutions and the Religious Consciousness," *Works,* VI, 39–96.

cated men and scholars; it can be accepted only by the uneducated, and theologians who persisted in teaching its doctrines must be considered equally ignorant. In Parker's
vocabulary "popular" was another word for "unenlightened."

The popular theology, with its idea of God and man, and of
their relation, is the philosophy of unreason, of folly. How can
you ask men of large reason, large conscience, large affections,
large love for the good God, to believe any one of the numerous
schemes of the Trinity, the miracles of the New or Old Testament; to believe in the existence of a devil whom God has made,
seeking to devour mankind? How can you ask such men to
believe in the existence of an angry God, jealous, capricious,
selfish, and revengeful, who has made an immeasurable hell
under his feet, wherein he designs to crowd down ninety-nine
thousand nine hundred and ninety-nine out of every hundred
thousand of his children? Will you ask Humboldt, the greatest
of living philosophers, to believe that a wafer is "the body of
God," as the Catholics say? or M. Comte, to believe that the
Bible is "the word of God," as the Protestants say? Will you
ask a man of great genius, of great culture, to lay his whole
nature in the dust, and submit to some little man, with no genius,
who only reads to him a catechism which was dreamed by some
celebate monks in the dark ages of human history? You cannot
expect such men to assent to that: as well might you ask the
whole solar system to revolve about the smallest satellite that
belongs to the planet Saturn.[3]

Modern science has shown that the theological astronomy, geol-
ogy, and geography are mixed with whims, which overlay their
facts; that the theological history is false in its chief particulars,
relating to the origin and development of mankind; that its
metaphysics are often absurd, its chief premises false; that the
whole tree is of gradual growth; and still men have the hardi-
hood to pretend it is all divine, all true, and that every truth in
the science and morals of our times, nay, any piety and benev-

3 "Of the Popular Theology of Christendom," *Works,* II, 159–160.

olence in human consciousness, has come from the miraculous revelation, and this alone! Truly it is a teacher's duty to expose this claim, so groundless, so wicked, so absurd, and refer men to the perpetual revelation from God in the facts of his world of matter and of man.[4]

Since religion is represented as thus unnatural and unreasonable, there are many [including some of the foremost among scholars and philosophers] who "sign off" from conscious religion altogether; they reject it, and will have nothing to do with it. It seems to war with their reason, with their conscience, their affections, their soul, and so far as possible they reject it.[5]

God's revelation to man has occurred not through miracles, but through "the facts of his world of matter and of man." Orthodoxy has been divorced from such enlightenment, from scholarship and scientific methodology, generally.

Parker's second criticism of popular theology is equally severe. The scheme is grossly inhuman; it has truly degraded human nature; and it has repeatedly subordinated man's soul to the "ambiguous, imperfect, and often erroneous Scriptures." It, consequently, condemns spontaneous gaiety; it sneers at common sense and the education of the understanding; it denounces the validity and authority of human reason. Because it recognizes no basis for religion in human nature and natural human powers, it imposes religion upon man by referring to authorities external to man's nature; this religion is therefore "unnatural" to man and hostile to his best nature. Moreover, it turns men against one another by its doctrine of "depravity" which calls man "a selfish and immortal devil, powerful only to sin, and immortal only to be eternally tormented." Parker concluded

4 "The Function of the Teacher of Religion," p. 303.
5 "Of the Popular Theology of Christendom," p. 159.

that according to the popular theology, man is God's failure.

All things which God made work well except human nature; and that worked so badly that it fell as soon as it was put together. God must start anew, and so he destroys all, except eight persons. But, so bad is human nature, the new family behave no better; they must be cast aside; and God discards all excepting the posterity of a single man. But they turn out as bad as the rest, and must be thrown over. No good comes of human reason and human nature; so at length "a new dispensation" is established. But the new dispensation has worked scarcely better than the others. The human race does not turn out as God designed or expected. It is a failure.[6]

Against these "popular" tenets with reference to human nature, Parker set up the contrary belief: that man *naturally* loves perfection, and that this natural love for perfection is the "causal principle" behind human striving. In the animal world there is no such striving; man alone is "partly his own providence," [7] and the development toward perfection of the human faculties is a fundamental aspect of the law of progress. That man can achieve his perfect end through the expansion of his several powers carries with it a metaphysical implication—that progress aims at individual differentiation.

I have tried to show there was a similar unity of life in the human race, pointing out the analogous progressive development of mankind from the state of ignorance, poverty, and utter nakedness of soul and sense, the necessary primitive conditions of the race, up to the present civilization of the leading nations. The primitive is a wild man, who gradually grows up to civilization. To me, the notorious facts of human history . . . admit of no other interpretation. . . . I have found a prophecy that what [man] wants is possible and shall one day be actual.[8]

[6] *Ibid.*, p. 142.   [7] "Human Progress," p. 287.
[8] "Experience as a Minister," pp. 333–335.

Thus, sentiments, ideas, and actions—the three stages in historical progress—indicate also the development related to the nature of man. Three stages in development are interpretive of the "notorious facts of human history"; by analogy they interpret also the development within man as he strives toward the perfection of his nature. The natural "love of perfection" in man is, therefore, like manliness; the elements in human nature strive toward, and finally achieve, perfect expression in the highest culmination of piety and religion. In general, Parker's position appears to parallel Adam Ferguson's emphasis on history as the continuous expression of man's attempt to adapt himself to new natural situations. But Parker's interpretation of adaptation is essentially religious, for he shifted the focus of the religious imagination from "the economy of redemption" after the Fall, to the progressive evolution of the human faculties toward God as the end of man's natural love for the perfect. Thus, progress and providence both begin in social solidarity and end in individual perfection and differentiation. But, the perfection which is achieved, according to Parker's theology, is the perfect expression of universal human judgments.

Parker often used the history of America to illustrate what he meant by progress in history and in human nature. He believed that the American historian should be a "prophetic patriot" and a "democrat," so that he might describe sympathetically the political progress of America; Parker believed that from the "scientific" viewpoint, democracy as "government of all, for all, and by all" [9] is the highest stage

9 "Hildreth's History of the United States," a review article of Richard Hildreth's *The History of the United States* (3 vols., New York, 1849); Parker's *Works,* VIII, 282.

of political development ever achieved in the history of mankind. He, therefore, believed that the historian should

trace the growth of the American people from their humble beginnings to their present condition to discover and point out the causes which have helped that growth, and the causes which have hindered it. To a philosophical historian this is no unpromising field; the facts are well known; it is easy to ascertain the ideas out of which the general political institutions of America have grown; it is not difficult to see the historical causes which have modified these institutions, giving them their present character and form. None but a democrat can thoroughly appreciate that history. As the history of Christianity must be written by a Christian, . . . so must the history of America be written by a democrat.[10]

This segment of universal history, the philosophy of progress applied to American institutions, illustrates, according to Parker, the initial struggle toward collectivism, and the final culmination of perfected individualism. Such individualism was interpreted by him as the establishment of political freedom.

The universe at large also provided Parker with evidence for the theory of progress. The law of evolutionary development toward perfection—which is illustrated in the history of religion, the gradual development of the human powers, and the establishment of free institutions—was interpreted as the basic characteristic of the natural order. Universal progress illustrates

the ascent from the lower and ruder to the higher and more comprehensive.[11]

10 *Works,* VIII, 274.
11 "The Conception of God in the Bible" (*Works,* VI, 99), the first in a series of four sermons usually referred to as Parker's "Longwood Sermons"; they were delivered on May 30 and 31, 1858, in the annual meeting of Progressive Friends, Longwood, Pennsylvania.

Ascending progress seems to be the general rule in the universe, things beginning in their lowest and humblest forms, and gradually going higher and higher, and becoming more complex.[12]

Each age is as sufficient to itself as any other age, the first as the last. The immense progress between the two is also the law of God, who has so furnished men that they shall find satisfaction for their wants, when they are babies of savage wildness and when they are grown men of civilization.[13]

These formulations are not fundamentally different from Spencer's. Both men recognized two basic aspects of the universal law: "ascending progress" and the change from the basically simple to the more complex. Furthermore, for Parker as well as for Spencer "all change is progress." Spencer stated the evolutionary theory as a universal law, for he included man's entire knowledge from physics to ethics as the validation of one comprehensive law of evolutionary change; he then combined this with the theory that evolution is the movement from "unified homogeneity" toward "differentiated heterogeneity." Spencer's fullest expression of his position, *Social Statics*, appeared—as did his other major works—too late for Parker to make use of them. He may have read some of the early articles, for he received a large collection of scientific writings during the 1850s, including the *Edinburgh Review* for which Spencer wrote his essay on "Progress, Its Law and Cause," as well as the application of the notion of progress to several important problems of natural history, social science, and universal history. In any case, both Parker and Spencer drew upon some of the same sources and set forth their findings in a similar manner.

[12] "The Relation of God and Man," p. 339.
[13] "The Natural and Philosophical Idea of God," the third sermon in the Longwood series; *Works*, VI, 146.

While he referred repeatedly to the areas which objectively illustrate or prove the law of progress, Parker used
this universal law primarily as the support for his fundamental theological teaching. The culmination of his theological views expresses most completely his characteristic
application of the theory of progressive evolution. Thus,
three factors which characterize the closing period of
Parker's career are interrelated: his deep disappointment
over the meagerness of America's moral development, his
interest in the increasing support given by the natural and
biological sciences to the theory of progressive evolution as
a universal law, and his renewed determination to present a
theology for absolute religion which would be accepted as
"the science of religion." [14] The third factor is central to
our present interest.

In his theology, Parker reemphasized and restated the
"three facts of man's religious consciousness" as the basis
for the corresponding "stages of religious experience."
Thus, the individual's religious experience also illustrates
the universal law of history; religiously, too, man proceeds
from sentiments, to ideas, and finally to action. In the first
stage, the individual consciousness encounters the sentiments of religion; these are formulated by the understanding so that they become ideas; participation, finally, in the
universal community is achieved, and the intellect's statement of individual sentiments are validated and acted upon.
Or, theologically phrased, the first stage of religious experience is the stage of self-consciousness; the second is the
development of the "idea" of God; the third stage is reached
when there is harmony in the relationship between God and
man. We have already outlined what Parker meant by self-

[14] "Ecclesiastical Institutions and Religious Consciousness," p. 44.

awareness in the context of his philosophy of religion. The second and third stages can be interpreted, according to Parker, as belonging to "theology" and to "religion."

Theology is devoted, therefore, to the development of the "conception" or "idea" of God. Parker's attention focussed again on the law of progress as he spoke of "the progressive development of the conception of God in the books of the Bible." Even in the span of years reflected by the composition of the Bible there is visible a distinct progress in man's idea of God.

What a change from Genesis to the Fourth Gospel. What a difference between the God who eats veal and fresh bread with Abraham, and commands him to make a burnt offering of his own son, who conveys all Palestine on such jocular tenure, and the God whom no man hath seen at any time; who is spirit and is to be worshipped in spirit and in truth; who is love, and who dwells with all loving and believing souls.[15]

The Bible, according to Parker, should be used as an indication of the progress which may still be expected as man's theological views continue to develop. To insist that "revelation" stopped with the end of the New Testament is, accordingly, impious: "It would be contrary to the spirit of Moses, and still more contrary to the spirit of Jesus, to attempt to arrest the theological and religious progress of mankind." [16] Though he emphasized "theological progress," he did not believe in the progressive evolution of God; he could not accept Hegel's idea of an "improvable and progressive deity." What he emphasized was the belief that theology, the intellectual part of religion, is subject to the law of progress. And, he attributed such progress in theology to his basic "causal principle"—the "natural love of

15 "The Conception of God in the Bible," p. 116.   16 *Ibid.*, p. 119.

perfection." He used it, in this context, to indicate man's constant striving in the formulation of an "idea" of God which more adequately corresponds to the objective counterpart of intellectual "love."

Parker recognized that this application of the law of progress to theology is incompatible with the "popular" theology of orthodoxy. The Christian sects pursue the "ecclesiastical method," accepting the Bible as the finished document of revelation, as the final truth and ultimate authority on all matters, and as the basis for *the* idea of God. In his sermon on "The Ecclesiastical Conception of God," Parker stated his belief that the popular theology is essentially static; it accepts the God of Genesis and arbitrarily makes its "primitive" theology serve the needs of men in the New England civilization of the nineteenth century. It excludes the thesis that theology develops; its God is ethically malicious and cruel; because it conceives of divine activity as spasmodic, its God is unsatisfactory to the needs of science; and, because God cannot be relied on, its theology is also inadequate to the religious needs of men.

With this rejection of the God of both the Bible and the Church, Parker turned to the dictates of natural reason for his "philosophical idea of God."

I . . . call this the philosophical or natural idea of God; . . . the philosophical idea, because derived by that [rational] method—the natural because it corresponds to nature.[17]

When a man pursues this natural, philosophic method of theology, takes his facts from consciousness in his own world, and observation in the world of matter, then he arrives at *the philosophical idea of the God of Infinite Perfection;* that God has all the qualities of complete and perfect being. . . . He has being without limitation. . . . He fills all spirit, not less

17 "The Natural and Philosophical Idea of God," p. 155.

than all matter, yet is not limited by either. . . . He is perfect cause, and perfect providence, creating all things from a perfect motive, of a perfect material, for a perfect purpose, and as a perfect means, and to a perfect end. So, of all conceivable worlds he makes the best possible, of all conceivable degrees of welfare he provides the best in kind and the greatest in bulk, not only for all as a whole, but for each as an individual. . . . There is no absolute evil in the world, either for the whole as all, nor for any one as part.

I think this idea of God as infinite perfection, perfect power, wisdom, justice, love, holiness, is the grandest thought which has ever come into mortal mind. It is the highest result of human civilization. Let no man claim it as his original thought; it is the result of all mankind's religious experience. It lay latent in human nature once, a mere instinctive religious feeling. At length it becomes a bright particular thought in some great mind; and one day will be the universal thought in all minds, and will displace all other notions of God.[18]

The Infinite Perfection of God . . . is the cornerstone of all my theological and religious teaching—the foundation, perhaps, of all that is peculiar in my system.[19]

This specific theological doctrine Parker interpreted as the universal "result of mankind's religious experience." It was initially a sentiment, vague and undefined. Through the intellectual powers of man it becomes a sharpened and formulated "idea." In the end it is accepted as a "universal" experience. Parker's theology was based on intellectual "analysis," which has gained the additional sanction of reason, and which has finally been confirmed and proved through "mankind's religious experience." It is therefore the theology of absolute religion; it supersedes all special theologies. While the early development of this idea is portrayed in the Biblical writings, the "finished" idea relies on

18 *Ibid.*, pp. 152–154.　　　　19 "Experience as a Minister," p. 330.

no external authority, whether tradition, Bible, or Church.
His theology is rooted in the educated and natural reason.
And, as a "proven" theology, it can serve the needs of ab-
solute religion.

Parker, therefore, interpreted his theology of the infinite
perfection as the theology which is "adequate." First,

to the purposes of science. First of all things the [natural] philosopher wants an adequate cause for the facts of the universe,
both the world of matter out of him, and the world of spirit in
him. He is to explain facts by showing their mode of operation,
and tracing them back to the cause—to the proximate cause
first, to the ultimate cause at last.

The God of infinite perfection is adequate cause for all the
facts of the universe.

The true idea of God is adequate to the purposes of science
both of matter and man.[20]

This conception is adequate too for the historian.

Then, too, how different will the great complex world of human
history appear! Men will study it without hindrance, asking
only for facts, for the law of the facts, and the human meaning
of the law. They will find no miracle in man's religious history;
but a continual development of a faculty common to all mankind, a gradual progress in religious feeling, religious thought,
religious act; no savage nation without consciousness of God, a
sense of dependence, obligation, gratitude; aye, and trust in
him, and something of love for him "even in savage bosoms"—
all this proportionate to the people's civilization. The philosopher will find God in all human history, in the gradual elevation of mankind from the low state of the wild man, to higher
and higher types of excellence.[21]

This theology is adequate, finally, "to the purposes of
religion."

20 "The Natural and Philosophical Idea of God," pp. 155, 157, 160.
21 Ibid., p. 159.

For that I want not merely a cause sufficient to my intellect, but much more. I want a God I can trust and have absolute confidence in, so that I am sure of him. . . . Soon as a man is considerably enlightened in his mind, conscience, heart, and soul, soon as he comprehends the power that is everywhere always, active and acting for good, then that savage deity is not enough for him. He wants not only infinite ability, . . . but also power of conscience, . . . and the infinite power of affection to love all men and all things. . . . Here it is in the true God of earth and heaven and human consciousness.[22]

The theology of God's infinite perfection is adequate to absolute religion, because religion relates man to God on the basis of trust and confidence; the "faithfulness" of God is underscored as the attribute of the divine, and "man is saved by God's faithfulness." This is the essence of absolute religion; the relationship of trust is universal, for it includes both creation and providence.

[God] stands related to us in two ways: first as the creative cause which brings us into being, either directly or remotely; second as the conservative providence which regulates the world and takes care that all goes right. . . . God's relation to man, causal and providential, must be perfect.[23]

Trust in God demands that we apply God's means, in God's way, for God's ends. That is what we are here for.[24]

While trust has ethical implications, Parker's characteristic interpretation is distinctly religious. He meant by the sense of "absolute security" that this is "what God owes to man; man has an absolutely inalienable right to the infinite providence of God."[25] Absolute religion is the "desire

22 *Ibid.*, pp. 160–161.
23 "The Relation of God and Man," pp. 329–330.
24 "Man in His Religious Aspects," *Works*, V, 345.
25 "Some Account of My Ministry," p. 58.

to be in harmony with the infinitely perfect God." [26] And, harmony is "love."

I cannot fail to love the infinite being who is above and within me, for to my mind he is the ideal wisdom and beauty, to my conscience the ideal justice and will, to my heart the ideal affection, and to my soul, the ideal integrity; the absolute God, perfect, good, just, and fair, the God who is in matter and spirit, and yet transcends them both with his infinity.[27]

These are the rewards of religion; they were spoken of by Parker as "the soul's normal delight in the infinite God." The most important result of human trust is the confidence in immortality. "The idea of immortality," he said, "belongs to the absolute religion; [it is] consistent with the infinite perfection of God." [28] While he advanced many arguments for the doctrine of immortality, he made it a matter ultimately of belief.

With the consciousness of immortality, with a certain knowledge of the infinite perfection of God, the perfect cause, the perfect providence, I can do all things; no doom is hopeless; disaster is the threshhold of delight.[29]

This theological principle was, nevertheless, also given an ethical meaning.

It is of great comfort to have in your soul a sure trust in immortality, of great value here and now to anticipate time and live today the eternal life. That we may all do. The joys of heaven will begin as soon as we attain the character of heaven and do its duties. That may begin today. It is everlasting life to know God; . . . try that, and prove its worth. Justice, usefulness, wisdom, religion, love are the best things we hope for in

[26] "The Relation of God and Man," p. 346.
[27] *Ibid.*, p. 347.
[28] *Sermons of Theism, Atheism, and the Popular Theology*, p. 269.
[29] *Ibid.*, p. 279.

heaven. Try them on; they will fit you here not less becomingly. They are the best things of earth. Think no outlay of goodness and piety too great. You will find your reward begin here. As much goodness and piety, so much heaven.[30]

Thus, the universals of heaven are available on earth. The rewards of absolute religion are initially personal; but its "delights" are finally universal. On the one hand, absolute religion follows the pattern of historical progress.

This religion which begins in the instinctive feelings, and thence advances to reflective ideas, assumes its ultimate form in the character of men, and so appears in their actions, individual, domestic, social, national, ecclesiastical, and general-human.[31]

On the other hand, absolute religion is interpreted as the movement from the simple "sense of dependence" to the universal "trust" in the God of infinite perfection.

What was it that Parker set out to accomplish in this theology of absolute religion? Several answers can be given. He attempted to contrast, first, several methods which are used as authorities for the theologies proposed. He contrasted the "ecclesiastical method" which is based on Biblical revelation with his "philosophical [or "rational"] method." Thus, while Emerson contrasted the Church with the soul, Parker placed his emphasis on the contrast between the Church and the natural reason. This suggests another difference between Emerson and Parker. But another answer to the question we have posed must also be given. Because of his use of the sense of dependence and human finitude, Parker's theology elaborated a view of God who may be referred to as "the adequate resting place of human finitude." This is why he emphasized "the infinity of

30 "Of Immortal Life"; *Works,* III, 345–346.
31 "Experience as a Minister," p. 336.

God," a term which the Enlightenment had popularized, and a doctrine basic to the theology associated with deism. And, those critics who spoke of his position as "vehemently deistical" were apparently justified. They had in mind his "rational" test of truth and his use of facts of experience to validate facts of consciousness. They recognized his insistence that the basis of religion and of morality must be sought in human nature and that this basis must then be validated in human experience. These articles of belief were not foreign to the deists: all truths must be considered unproved which are above or beyond reason; what is believed without proof belongs to primitive superstition; to rid one's self of superstitions is to be free; the rational mind, therefore, is the liberated mind, for it has freed its concepts of superstition. And, Parker had separated the "transient" from the "permanent" aspects of Christianity; the "permanent" in religion, or absolute religion, was even more extreme than the position of the deists. The "absolute" which Parker outlined superseded even "natural theology." He believed that only true religion—the love of the infinite and perfect God, and the love of infinitely perfectible man—is absolute, and that no theology is ultimate.

His universal and absolute religion was given its support on the grounds of human nature. And, his theology of the God of infinite perfection is fundamentally a rephrasing of his conception of the infinite perfectibility of man. Condorcet's *The Progress of the Human Mind* (1793) was the culmination of the Enlightenment's view of progress; it emphasized the faith in universal history as the illustration of the progress of the human mind. Condorcet's summary is strikingly like Parker's position: "No bounds have been fixed to the improvement of the human faculties; . . . the perfectibility of man is absolutely indefinite." This statement of the perfectibility of man as the indefinite improvement of human powers is essentially the same as Parker's. He, nevertheless, viewed it theologically, and thus the two related doctrines have their affinity with the fundamental teachings of the Enlightenment, and Parker's critics were not wholly in error when they interpreted his position as "deistical." He would, nevertheless, have denied it. He said that his doctrine of the infinity of God and the perfectibility of man were principles basic to "speculative" and "practical" *theism,* not to natural theology. This distinction is important in many respects. Parker, though he believed in the natural religion fundamental to deism, based his universal and absolute religion on *human nature,* not on the pervasive laws that order natural events. He rejected distinctions which separated natural from revealed religion, and would have agreed substantially with Tillotson's statement that "natural religion is the foundation of all revealed religion." He emphasized the relationship between creation and providence, but he did not conceive of providence as the operation of perfectly mechanical laws nor did he look to nature for the evidence of God. He unrelentingly criticized the popular theology, but he did not make it his aim to destroy all historic Christianity in the interest of "natural" religion, nor did he wish to rescue religion from bondage to the primitive only to return it to an original simplicity and purity; his gospel of "essential" Christianity was a reconstructed Gospel, and his absolute religion was interpreted as the highest and most advanced stage of religious development. Thus, while his doctrines of "the infinity of God" and "the infinite perfectibility of man" were taken over from the Enlightenment, and while he, like the deists, believed that the universals have an a priori foundation, his position was not merely a restatement of naturalistic deism for the nineteenth century, but a humanism and humanitarianism based on human nature and history.

His theology of absolute religion was intended to be an "educated" theology. He said that it depends on neither a scholastic, an ecclesiastic, or a transcendental philosophy. But, independent of all schools of theology, and based only on the natural reason and the rational understanding of human nature, Parker's theology purported to be a "critical human science" and a theological position adequate to the needs of science, history, and universal religion. It is the culmination of the critical philosophy of Theodore Parker.

Chapter 5

CONCLUSION

O UR EXAMINATION of the critical theology and philosophy of Theodore Parker leads to several conclusions regarding the extent to which he embraced New England transcendentalism. His investigations of the Old and New Testaments with the help of critical tools, his emphasis on the rational and historical basis for religion, and his enunciation of the theology of "the infinite perfection of God" and "the infinite perfectibility of man" illustrate most clearly his characteristic methods and interests. These are the areas which best reveal where Parker stood with respect to his contemporaries; his theological formulations epitomize his viewpoint. Emerson spoke of him as "our Savanarola," while William Gannett added that, on the basis of his "system," "Parker was the Paul of transcendentalism." [1] We are not misled, therefore, when we look to his theology for an estimate of his "faith" in the transcendentalist "gospel."

From this viewpoint our basic conclusion is that Parker represents "a transitional figure." He attempted to "mediate" between, and thereby reconcile, opposing extremes. His extensive use of the works of German critical theologians for his study of Biblical writings and historical Christian doctrines supports this view. Parker relied on the

[1] Quoted in E. D. Mead, *The Influence of Emerson* (Boston, 1903), p. 111.

scholars who stated the position for the "mediating" school in German theology.

The first generation of nineteenth century German theologians were divided into three main groups. At one extreme were the rationalists, the vigorous opponents of all supernaturalism. The most influential figure in this group was Heinrich Eberhard Gottlob Paulus, who taught at Heidelberg from 1811 to 1844, and whose *Life of Jesus* is a typical expression of the extreme rationalism of his day. At the other extreme was confessional orthodoxy of the most uncompromising kind; it had a notable representative in Ernest Wilhelm Hengstenberg, professor in Berlin from 1826 until his death in 1869. Between these extremes was the group which had been influenced by Schleiermacher's warmth of faith and his acceptance of many of the results of higher criticism, by Hegel's dialectic as applied to development in history, and by the historical interpretations of Barthold Georg Niebuhr. Johann Neander had been Schleiermacher's most promising student; his life work on *The History of the Christian Religion and Church*, as well as his oft-repeated phrase, "the heart makes the theologian," are evidences of the profound influence of Schleiermacher. Another scholar who combined with his Pietistic sympathies an acceptance of critical interpretations was Friedrich August Tholuck, who turned Halle from the rationalism of his predecessor Wolff to the Evangelicalism which characterized it during the remainder of the century. A somewhat more conservative, but equally critical, representative of the central group was Isaac August Dorner. More radical, and intensively Hegelian, was F. C. Baur who used the dialectical triad to interpret the fundamental aspects of first-century Christianity. The other Tübingen critical theologian, D. F. Strauss, was equally familiar with the Hegelian philosophy, but he combined with it Niebuhr's principles of historical analysis as he stated his mythical interpretation of "the life of Jesus." Wilhelm M. L. De Wette, who in addition to his critical study of both the Old and New Testaments also examined the history of Christian doctrine, belonged also to this group of German theologians.

Because of his wide reading, many have tended to exaggerate the divergent "influences" upon Parker. It is clear, however, that the works of this critical group were central, and that he interpreted for America a "mediating" theology. It avoided both extreme rationalism and Evangelical orthodoxy. His *Introduction* to the Scriptures for his generation in America "mediated" between these extremes; it was radical when viewed from the standpoint of New England orthodoxy, but his conclusions, while advanced, were not extreme in their individualist emphasis.

His philosophy of religion was "transitional." Its basic outline was traced, as we have noted, during a controversy between the extreme orthodoxy of Norton, based on empiricism, and Emerson's equally extreme emphasis on the individual reason and the "authentic" insights of the individual soul. That Parker should have stated a more complete and rational system of "spiritual philosophy" than is to be found in the transcendentalism of Emerson's *Divinity School Address*, is, as we have seen, due to the greater role assumed in his philosophy by the understanding and the study of human experience in history. If spiritual truths written in the human soul are to be discovered invariably through a mere act of volition, as the more subjective transcendentalists would have us believe, there is certainly no

need for elaborating a philosophy of human nature and of
human history. Parker did not flee to the camp of the empiricists; they have, he said, only particulars and no universals. But, he also did not accept fully Emerson's emphasis on the individual's "authentic" insights discovered
through the soul. By his view of the understanding, his
belief that "judgments *a priori*" must be validated also as
"facts of history," and his general emphasis on "universals"
and the history of mankind, Parker explicitly criticized
Emerson's position; there is a significant contrast between
his analysis of human nature or his emphasis on the objective grounds of universals, and Emerson's subjective and
individualistic emphasis. Parker was conscious of the contrast; he stated it in this way: "We once heard of a man
who thought everything was in the soul, and so gave up all
reading, all continuous thought. Said another, 'If all is in
the soul, it takes a *man* to find it.' " [2] Emerson's man was
the individual, while Parker's was the "real man." This suggests again that Parker's view, as seen from the vantage
point of his philosophy of religion, was mediating. He never
hesitated to criticize the theology based on "the ecclesiastical method," but he did not contrast the Church with the
individual soul. He believed that the inductive and deductive methods are supplementary, that the judgments of
reason are validated empirically through the scientific
study of historical data, that "facts of intuition" are not
incompatible with the concepts of the understanding. When
he did, on occasion, utilize the "transcendental appeal," he
considered it inadequate until it was validated by generic

[2] *Critical and Miscellaneous Writings, the Collected Works of Theodore Parker, edited by Frances Power Cobbe* (London, 1867), X, 220–
221.

human experience. Thus, in his philosophy, Parker "mediated" between the critical and objective approach and the more subjective emphasis of the transcendental temper. Parker marks the transition from the Enlightenment to transcendentalism, and from eighteenth to nineteenth century thinking.

His theological view substantiates this position. There were striking similarities between his theology of "the infinity of God" and "the infinite perfectibility of man" and the naturalistic emphasis of Enlightenment deism. He nevertheless criticized deists for their mechanistic interpretation of the natural order. His striking emphasis on "absolute religion" as the religion of *human* nature, as well as of the "world of matter," shows the contrast between his view and the theology of deism. But, Parker was equally critical of the transcendentalists, who, he said, "take *all* their facts from their own consciousness." [3] Parker's theology was, therefore, neither naturalistic, nor intuitionistic; it was naturalistic only to the extent that Parker stressed *human* nature; it was intuitionistic only to the extent that universals are "legitimated" by the reason, which waits on the understanding's "proper" functioning. James Freeman Clarke called his position "natural theism," as accurate a description as may be possible. He used "weapons of science" to destroy "the popular theology," but he meant by this phrase higher criticism, historical study, and the analysis of human nature. He underscored a naturalistic interpretation of the institutions and sacraments of Christianity, but he made a philosophy of human nature the basis of his theology. His entire system moved from demonstrative certainty to the practical "stages" of reli-

[3] "God in the World of Man," p. 272.

gious experience; from proofs for God's existence to forms
of the experience of God. His critical use of the theory of
progress was valuable to him as a philosophy of history, but
he translated this Enlightenment emphasis into theological
terms; the indefinite perfectibility of the human faculties
became the basis for his view of the infinite perfection of
God. Thus, in his theology, too, Parker elaborated a "mediating" position. He stands between the characteristic Enlightenment views and the greater emphasis on human
consciousness of the transcendentalists.

We said at the outset that this is our fundamental question: to what extent did Theodore Parker embrace New
England transcendentalism? Our answer to this question
has been stated in various ways. From the viewpoint of the
Divinity School Address, and on the basis of direct statements taken from reviews and correspondence, Emerson
and Parker are contrasting figures. Parker was unwilling
to accept the extreme individualism of Emerson. Another
contrast is apparent in their treatments of human nature.
Emerson emphasized the personal soul and its revelations;
the human soul was viewed as a "microcosm" of nature, and
its individual principles have, therefore, direct validity.
Parker, on the other hand, emphasized the universals of human nature, and their authentication in common human
experience. Human nature, in the developmental process,
was what Parker idealized. He is, therefore, nearer evolutionism than transcendentalism. Parker's emphasis on history, both as a "scientific" discipline and as the area which
substantiates the judgments of reason, suggests another
contrast between his viewpoint and Emerson's transcendentalism. Emerson placed no predominant stress on historical studies, and he did not look to history for validation

of the soul's "insights." Parker stood near, but not within, New England transcendentalism. He looked upon Emerson's as an "extreme" viewpoint; his "spiritual philosophy" is consequently a critical system. He cannot be referred to, therefore, simply as "Emerson's disciple"; his acceptance of Emerson's viewpoint was, literally, half-hearted. In his critical theology and philosophy, Parker depended primarily on the experience of mankind in history, and on the objective study of the nature of man, for the validation of the universals "given" to man. He was primarily concerned that his views be "adequate" to history, science, and religion.

Appendix

THE PREVIOUS QUESTION
between
MR. ANDREWS NORTON AND HIS ALUMNI
Moved and Handled in a Letter
to All Those Gentlemen
BY LEVI BLODGETT

Boston, 1840

Gentlemen,

If the subjects you are debating concerned simply the two respectable persons who alone, as yet, have taken part in the discussion, the public would not have listened to their words; nor should I have troubled your wisdom with this letter. But the matter before you is one of wide and deep concernment, which affects the whole community. You therefore, I doubt not, will pardon a plain man for addressing a few words, to your respectful consideration. The humble style, and perhaps uncouth phraseology of my letter, I trust, you will candidly excuse, when I assure you that "ower much o' my life has been spent at the plough, and ower little at the college or the schule." I am but an obscure man; my name, I think, is strange to your ears. But I have interests at issue which depend on the question you are debating.

Our age, Gentlemen, as Mr. Norton so acutely remarks, is one of movement and transition. Great questions which the world had previously passed upon and settled, come up to receive a new solution. "Terrible questions," as some one says, "are raised by human Reason," and matters taken for granted hitherto, or decided by authority that is merely personal, now solicit rejudgment, by which, in some cases, it seems likely that former decisions may be set aside. I perceive by the Pamphlets of Mr. Norton and his Alumnus, that several questions are now before you, which these two gentlemen are discussing in a manner, scholarlike in some measure, and able no doubt; but not in the most scientific manner, as I look at the thing. But this is the fault of the circumstances which led to the discussion, and is by no means a reproach to either party; especially if we consider how little scientific discussion on theological and religious subjects has hitherto taken place in this country. But I can make no pretensions to discuss *scientifically* such lofty matters; I wish only to offer a few thoughts in my own homely way.

If I understand the Pamphlets of Mr. Norton and his Alumnus, there are now two subjects before you, which have grown incidentally out of the discussion on the latest form of Infidelity.

1. There is the great vital question, *Do men believe in Christianity* SOLELY *on the ground of miracles?* I say SOLELY, for unless miracles are held to be the sole ground of accepting it, the question is only one of the more or less; and therefore is of little theological importance, since it concerns individual experience alone, and is not to be settled by theological science, but by the personal biography of each Christian. To decide upon the sole evidence of the Christian Religion, Christianity, as it is conceived of in the mind, must be subjected to a rigid analysis, whereby its truths shall be separated from the evidence on which those truths are accepted. This evidence must then itself be analyzed into its essential and accidental constituent parts; and, if I understand the matter, one party says by the test of his philosophy and experience, the ultimate result of the last analysis, will be miracles: while the other separates miracles as something adventitious and regards them as foreign substances, by no means a necessary ingredient of that evidence and still less the very essence of it. The truth itself is its own evidence, the Alumnus would say, and God's truth cannot be made more obligatory or effective by any miracles; still less does it derive its sanction from them.

2. The next *is a literary question,* which "parteth itself into

four heads," that relate respectively to the theological character of Spinoza, Schleiermacher, and De Wette, and some errors, supposed or real, about translating. The last is a pedagogical question, to be passed upon by linguists; and might well enough, I reckon, be postponed indefinitely, or laid before a bench of schoolmasters for decision. It seems a pity that our Salmasius and Milton should quarrel, even amicably, about parts of speech. The historical and literary question respecting the distinguished scholars above named, is one which does not much concern the church or the community, wherein Mr. Norton says "there is no controlling power of the intellect," which alone can settle that question. It is a pity these men should attract the discussion, out of its proper channel, to themselves. If they were respectively atheists, disbelievers in the personality of God, and the miracles of the New Testament, they are certainly not the only atheists and disbelievers, and perhaps are not the worst. I take it, few Christians would solicit a comparison with these three men; I do not mean in respect to sharp-sightedness, or insight into matters of philosophy and theology, but in respect to a Christian life. Now if their lives were the natural result of their principles and sentiments, as they must have been, if a corrupt tree cannot bring forth good fruit; I would say God send us more such men, and may their influence extend wide and deep. But perhaps we are misinformed as to the character of these men, though it is hardly a common vice to exaggerate the virtues of men we do not agree with. But why should this literary question be discussed, before the public are ready for it? The works of these gentlemen are but little known among us. I take it for granted that one party in this debate had never read the chief works of Spinoza before this controversy began; and the other thinks not ten persons in the neighborhood had read them. The works of the two other scholars are but little read in this country, as the booksellers tell me. Even the language is not much known, for I take it they are written in German, and have not been translated except a few fragments published in Reviews. Now books cannot do much harm unless they are read. I should think, therefore, Gentlemen, that it would be as well to drop this subject also, until other matters more pressing shall first be despatched.

Gentlemen, I will now venture to recall your attention to the first subject, THE SOLE EVIDENCE OF CHRISTIANITY; the only subject of real moment. But since this matter is embarrassed with difficulties not easily removed, I will put forth a few thoughts on the PREVIOUS QUESTION, which I think must be decided before we touch the evidence of Christianity. This previous question is as follows: HOW DO MEN COME TO HAVE ANY RELIGION, or, in other words, *on what evidence do they receive the plainest religious truths?* Gentlemen, we must settle the *genus,* before we decide upon the *species.* The evidence for religious truths in *general,* I take it, cannot be different in *kind,* from the evidence for the *special* religious truths of Christianity. For as all religions contain some truths—on which alone they rest—that are identical with some truths in Christianity, and therefore not hostile to that religion, for one truth can never be hostile to another, inasmuch as God's kingdom is not divided against itself; and since religious belief and conviction are, substantially, the same thing in all minds, Heathen or Christian, so it follows incontestably, that there must be the same *kind* of evidence to induce belief and conviction in both cases, as men's minds and hearts are at bottom the same. I do not see how there can be two *kinds* of evidence, any more than two kinds of *right;* but you, Gentlemen, are learned, and can settle difficulties that puzzle simple folks. However, there may be different *quantities* of evidence in the two cases, as the quantity of *truth* may differ in two religions, or the quantity of religious *belief* and *conviction* in two individuals of the same or of different religions.

Now *on what evidence do men admit the primary and essential truths of all religions?* Among these primary truths, I take it, are A BELIEF IN THE EXISTENCE OF GOD, and A SENSE OF DEPENDENCE ON HIM. I call these *primary* and *essential* truths, because without them I cannot conceive any religion possible. I reckon that man is by nature a religious being; i.e., that he was made to be religious, as much as an ox was made to eat grass.

The germs of religion, then, both the germs of religious principle and religious sentiment, must be born in man, or innate, as our preacher says. *The existence of God* is a fact given in our nature: it is not something discovered by a process of reasoning; by a long series of deductions from facts; nor yet is it the last generalization from phenomena observed in the universe of mind or matter. But it is a truth fundamental in our nature; given outright by God; a truth which comes to light as soon as self-consciousness begins. Still further, I take *a sense of dependence on God,* to be a natural and essential sentiment of the soul, as much as feeling, seeing, and hearing, are natural sensations of the body. Here, then, are the religious instincts which lead man to God and religion, just as naturally, as the intellectual instincts lead him to truth, and animal instincts to his food. Here, then, is a correspondence between the nature of man, and the nature of the whole universe wherewith one becomes acquainted. As there is light for the eye; sound for the ear; food for the palate; friends for the affections; beauty for the imagination; truth for the reason; duty for conscience, so there is God for the religious sentiment, or sense of dependence on Him. Now all these presuppose one another; as a want essential to the structure of man's mind or body, presupposes something to satisfy it. And as the sensation of hunger presupposes food to satisfy it, so the sense of dependence on God, presupposes his existence and character; though from this sense, taken in its philosophical nakedness, the unity of God, could not, perhaps, be inferred, and certainly the personality, or impersonality of God would in no wise follow.

Now I shall attempt to prove the existence of a religious nature, and also the existence of these two primary and essential truths of religion in man.

1. *Negatively, by an argument fetched from the logical absurdity involved* in the opposite doctrine that man has *not* a religious nature, or has not the primary truths of religion innate in him. I take it for granted on all hands, that religion is needed for the harmonious growth and welfare of man; that without it, this life would be, as somebody says, "poor, and brutish, and

nasty, and short"; that without God and religion, man's better nature, his higher reason, and spiritual powers, would be what the eye would become without light, the ear without sound, and the affection without friends. Now it is absurd to suppose God should create man thus dependent on God and on religion, and not give him power in himself to become perfectly assured in his own heart, of the existence of God, and his sustaining power on which we may depend. It is no more absurd and revolting, to suppose that in some other part of the universe he has created an order of beings, with a man's appetite for food, but with no powers of procuring that food. All animals are perfectly suited by their natures, to the sphere they move in, and it is absurd, and even impious, to suppose man is an exception to this law, and that while instincts supply his perishing body, there are no similar, but higher instincts to supply his undying soul.

2. The existence of these truths, and this religious nature, may be shown philosophically *by an analysis of the powers of the soul.* You find the *belief in God* as an indestructible element of the human soul. You come back to this fact as you examine and analyze any faculty of our nature. Take the tendency to seek for a cause in the effect; it leads straight to the supreme or absolute Cause, a knowledge of which is presupposed as the foundation of all finite causes. Take the sense of the Beautiful; you come to the idea and arche-type of infinite Loveliness, the altogether-Beautiful. Take the moral emotions, you come immediately to the eternal Right as it speaks through Conscience. Take the affections, you return to him who is Love. Thus in these, and in all other departments of the soul (so to say), you come back to the primal Truth; the light of all our being; to God. And you see the truth of the statement, "In him we live and move and have our being."

Analyze the religious feelings, hopes, and opinions as they now exist in you; separate whatever is not essential to the idea of religion; what is merely individual and peculiar to yourself or your sect, and you come back to a *sense of dependence on God* as the ultimate result of the last analysis. This you find given in the soul. Man feels that he is poor, and weak, and blind, and naked, and admits the truth, "without Thee we can do nothing, and are nothing." I do not say this sense of dependence would lead you to a *personal* God. It will not disclose to you the nature of God; more than the eye discloses the nature of light; the ear that of sound; or the hand that of matter. A knowledge of the nature of God is not more essential to religion, than knowledge of the nature of light, sound, and matter, is essential to seeing, hearing, or touching. The hand discovers to you something that resists its touch; this sense of dependence discovers to you something on which you must, and may depend, but what in the one case resists, and in the other supports, neither the hand, nor this sense of dependence can, in any wise, discover to you.

3. The same thing may be proved experimentally, *by an argument fetched from history.* You find no nation, civilized or savage, which does not admit the existence of God, and the sense of dependence upon Him. This fact is so notorious, that I shall present no proofs thereof to "learned clerks" like yourselves. It would not be necessary to prove it, even to simple folks like my own companions and neighbors. The only exceptions to this belief are *professed atheists;*—but this exception disturbs no one, it only confirms the rule,—and *men who grow up in perfect seclusion* from all human beings. The latter, I will admit, give no indication of possessing the idea of God, or the sense of dependence on Him. But any argument hostile to my position, derived from this source, is met by the *statement,* that these germs are probably there, only they have never had those social influences, which are the necessary occasions of awakening them and the germs of other high faculties of the soul. The subsequent history of these wretched persons, proves the truth of the *statement.* Such an argument is repelled by the *fact,* that these men neither laugh nor speak articulate language, and yet no one contends, from that circumstance, that the tendency to laugh and speak is not innate in man, though dependent on certain conditions and occasions for its active development.

I am well aware, Gentlemen, that some of you will say in opposition to this argument, that a miraculous revelation of the primary and essential truths of religion was made to man from without, and through the senses, by his Creator, at any early period of the world, which revelation has been propagated by tradition, ever since. Now when historical evidence of the fact, antecedently so improbable, is laid before me, it will be soon enough to point out the fault which vitiates and destroys your whole argument, viz., that such a revelation from without could not be made to man and receive by him, except on the supposition that these germs were innate. An outward revelation could only be the *occasion* of manifesting these germs, and not the cause of religion in man. It cannot be the creation of a new element in man; as it must be if these germs are not already in him—it could only be the awakening of an element, that still slept.

Now the progress and development of religion in man, I take it, is after this wise: the religious instincts, which ally us to God,—like the animal instincts, which connect us with matter—must needs display themselves in action, as the other higher faculties of man come into full life. The various objects of nature, and events of life, and intercourse of man with man, furnish an occasion for wakening all the faculties. In a rude society religion will have but a low development, and assume a rude form. As the tribe or race improves, the manifestations of religion becomes more perfect. The form changes to suit the culture of the age. Of course various forms of worship, or "systems of religion," will prevail, corresponding to the peculiarities of the race, its character, condition and culture.

Such being the origin of religion in man, it is advanced as other human interests are. At the head of all departments of human thought, or interest, stand individuals, who are in some measure the concrete type of that interest. Thus for example, in Legislation there are Minos and Moses; Homer in Poetry; Phidias in Sculpture; and in later times Raphael, Mozart, Bacon, and Newton in their respective spheres. All the great interests of mankind are carried forward by distinguished individuals. In the humbler affairs of agriculture, war, and politics, these individuals are numerous, for many will enter a department which lies level to the wishes and abilities of the many. But in the higher regions of human thought, these guides and types are less numerous and of a nobler stature. This rule holds good in Poetry and Philosophy. Mankind has many leaders in war, and but few great creative artists, and profound philosophers, because many can fight, and but few exercise the creative imagination, or think profoundly. Now as the religious interest is the very highest possible interest of man, he must expect fewer leaders and types in this, than in any other department of human concern. There are an hundred warriors who rule over the body by force, to one philosopher who rules in the mind by thought; and perhaps an hundred such to one creative, original, religious teacher, who rules through the heart by his superior holiness and faith; by his clearer vision of divine things which comes of his more complete obedience to "the law of the Spirit of life."

Now these original religious teachers do not derive their authority or their truths from themselves. The higher we ascend in human interests, the less is there of personal, and the more of divine authority. The religious teachers confess they derive their truths from God, and come not of themselves. Now I take it, all men have two *direct* channels of communication with God, viz., Conscience and the religious Sentiment, that is, the moral and religious powers of man; his two highest and most permanent faculties, which are not accidental, but essential and of course immortal. I call them channels of *direct* communication with God, because I can find nothing interposed between Conscience and God, or between Him and the religious Sentiment; we border closely upon God everywhere; here we touch and he interpenetrates us, if I may so speak. Conscience and the religious Sentiment, I reckon, are to the soul, what the ear and the eye are to the body. One reveals the moral law; the other the Beauty of Holiness, and excellency of Divine Things. We have besides numerous *indirect* ways of communicating with God; the Senses lead to Him through sensible things; the Understanding through effects; the Imagination through beautiful objects; and the Affections through friends. Here the communication is mediate, as in the other it is without mediators; these two streams of moral and religious Truth flow direct from God, the primitive fountain of all Rectitude and Holiness. Now in most men, these two channels, to continue the figure, are obstructed by sensuality and sinfulness. Not one man in a myriad has his conscience so active as his eye. Few deem it trustworthy, like the ear, or the hand. Not one in a million perhaps has his religious Sentiment so active and efficient as the bodily senses. Consequently these men, though they may know much of the outer world, of things seen and handled; though they may understand their laws, and *use,* and perhaps sometimes catch a glimpse of their *meaning* likewise, can know little of the vast world of moral and religious Truth; little of God. Their Deity is "a God afar off"; whose very existence is a matter of reasoning and inference, of which they can never be quite certain. Their sense of duty is weak; their consciousness of God is feeble. Their confidence in duty and religion therefore, on common occasions, cannot be relied on; yet by a beautiful characteristic of our nature, in times of peril, this degraded religious Sentiment will sometimes arise, assert its right and support the man who has so long been false thereto.

Now as these guides of mankind, in Poetry, War, Philosophy, Music or the Arts, were men, highly gifted by God with powers for their several callings, which powers they improved by use, and sharpened by intense love of their vocation,—so in religious interests, the guides of our race are men highly gifted by God at the first, who obey the fundamental law of their nature, and not only have indirect communication with God, through natural objects, but immediate connection through these two channels, which they have never closed up, by their sensuality and sin. These men move religion forward and upwards, as humbler geniuses promote and elevate humbler interests. These men create new religions and make religious epochs. They are enlightened directly from God, for the religious sentiment and conscience, "his greater and lesser light," shine straight into them. It is no figure of speech to say these men are inspired. They speak from this divine inspiration to the souls of men, and souls obey; at first slowly and reluctant, at last with servile homage and prostrate adoration. There is so much divine in them—viewed from the stand of the world,—that it is said they cannot be men, so they are confounded with Divinity itself. Hence these men are deemed gods, and so become objects of worship. Their influence on the world is immense; far greater than that of chieftains or sages. They turn a deep, wide furrow through the stubborn soil of human selfishness and sin, and wholesome grains, and heavenly flowers, and living groves mark where their name has passed. You find such men at the beginning of each religious epoch. But though inspired, their inspiration is no more strange and out of the way, than that of the Poet or the Painter, the Philosopher, or the Artist; it is only higher, and greater in degree, and more intense in its action. Yet though possessed of a greater measure of inspiration than other great souls, like them, they are not perfectly above all that is national, local, temporary, or even personal to themselves. Religious truth is imparted to men gradually as they are able to bear it. Absolute truth and absolute religion are not for men who are subject to the various peculiarities of their nation, place and age, and to their own idiosyncracies. Now as these latter perpetually change, the old form of religion, unable to change with them, gradually becomes obsolete. A new teacher of religion arises; starts from a higher stand and separating the peculiarities of the old form which adapted it to its age, climate and nation—constructs a new form suitable to the altered condition of mankind, which shall, for its season, carry forward the good work, until "in the fulness of time," it gives place to somewhat higher and better.

Now mankind obeys these teachers because it sees and feels the truth they bring, and the superiority of their gifts, for these men say what others would gladly say, but cannot. The divinity of an inspired and original religious teacher is seen and appreciated as men see and appreciate the superior talents of Alexander or Hannibal. It required no miracle to convince the centurion or the common soldier, that Caesar was a greater man than himself, and possessed more martial skill. It required no miracle to teach the warblers of Ionia or Thebes that Homer or Pindar sang sweeter than they. Now as in these cases, men judge in their own minds of the poetic power, and military prowess of Homer and Caesar, requiring no foreign proof thereof, nor dreaming of any test, but the works of those men; so in the case of a religious teacher men listen to Zoroaster, or Budha, or Fo, feeling the superiority of these men, and believing the truth which is offered, as a part of their birth-right too long kept from them.

But there is still a further consideration to be attended to. It may be said "these religious teachers pretended to work miracles." I would not deny that they *did* work miracles. If a man is obedient to the law of his mind, conscience and heart, since his intellect, character and affections are in harmony with the laws of God, I take it, he can do works, that are impossible to others who have not been so faithful, and consequently are not "one with God" as he is; and this is all that is meant by a miracle. But while this must be admitted, both as a logical conclusion and a historical fact—for without it we cannot account for the wide-spread belief in such miracles, that does not spring out of dreams or lies, which, themselves, would require explanation likewise—I must confess myself unable to determine the kind, or the number of miraculous acts performed by any one of these religious teachers. The miraculous power of Zoroaster and Elijah, has doubtless been exaggerated; for men whose senses are more active than their souls, find it more easy to cite a visible and monstrous fact as evidence of a man's superiority, than trust to the less tangible fact of his superior character, more celestial sentiments and thoughts. Hence legends, (or *mythi*—I think the learned call them) relating the acts of a religious teacher, increase in number, and marvellousness, in proportion to the sensuality of the people where they originate, or in proportion to their ignorance of the facts of the case. The histories of Zoroaster offer a good illustration of this statement, which is proved true also by the difference between the canonical gospels, and apocryphal writings, which latter originated in a later age, and among a people more ignorant of the facts of Christ's life. Now the possession of this miraculous power, when it can be proved, as I look at the thing, is only a *sign* (which may be uncertain) of the superior genius of a religious teacher, or a *sign* that he will utter the truth, and never a *proof* thereof. Consequently, it offers no more valid evidence of the excellence of a religion, than it would offer for the excellence of a poem or philosophy.

Religion—thus *caused* by the innate germs thereof, in the soul; thus *occasioned* by the outer world; thus *promoted* by inspired men,—when active and powerful in the community, affects the various faculties of the soul. It posseses the understanding and forms a creed; the fancy and creates a legendary tale; the moral sense and consciousness of sin, and produces rites. It affects the heart and forms a symbol.

Now if such is the origin, and growth of religion in general, we may perhaps apply these results to the special case of Christianity. Gentlemen, Christianity is one religion among several others. One species of a numerous class. It must therefore agree in some features with all other religions with the grossest worship of nature, and the most refined deism; otherwise it might be *Christianity,* but could not be religion, for I hold it to be granted that there can be but one *kind* of religion, though it may exist in various degrees of purity and intensity, and under the most various forms. Thus there is but one kind of *water,* though it may be more or less pure as it is less or more combined with foreign matter, and in different places, may exist in various quantities, and in various forms, as frozen to ice, or sublimated to an invisible vapor. Now I reckon true Christianity to be the highest form of religion. The Christianity of the church is, gentlemen—you know better than I what the Christianity of the church is,—what is the average morality and religion of the community, and therefore of the church, which only subsists by representing and slightly idealizing that average morality and religion. But the Christianity of Christ is the purest, the most intense, and perfect religion ever realized on earth. I say *realized* for it was realized in its arche-type and founder, though perhaps never since then. I will not say it is absolute religion—and therefore that Christ is the ultimate incarnation of God, for I cannot measure the counsels of the Infinite. I have not "*firm* footing in the clouds," as some pretend to have. But for myself, I can conceive of no higher religion than Christianity, as I understand it. I do not mean the Christianity of Calvin or Luther; of the Unitarians or the Quakers; of Paul, James or Peter or John, all of which are obviously one-sided and in part false—but the Christianity of Jesus. I can conceive of no man who shall more fully represent the moral and religious side of our nature; none who shall receive more fully direct religious and moral inspiration from God, and therefore no more perfect moral and religious incarnation of God, than Jesus of Nazareth. Therefore I can assent to Paul's statement, "In him dwelleth all the fulness of the Godhead." Supposing that Paul did not mean to say Jesus represented any but the moral and religious side of our nature. Homer is a type of poetry; Socrates of thought, and in their several departments they surpass Jesus, who was neither a poet nor a philosopher. God creates the "perfect man" fractionally, and we can only construct the pure ideal of man, historically, by selecting the essential attributes from many celestial souls. It was from five hundred fair maidens that Phidias sought absolute loveliness, and formed his eclectic statue of ideal beauty. But even if some man should be created in the full measure of perfect humanity—and should unite the poetic, philosophic, artistic, political and religious archetypes in himself, he would, it is true, be a more perfect incarnation of God, than Jesus was; for the sum-total of his being would be greater and equally pure; but yet he would not be a more perfect manifestation of incarnation of ideal moral and religious excellence than Jesus. Of course he could not reveal a more perfect religion, as I take it. But I would not insist on this conclusion, where it is so easy to make mistakes.

I am content, in the rest of this letter, to take it for granted that Christianity is absolute religion; perfect religion; the sentiment and principle; the harmony of morality and religion, united and made life. It is religion not limited by creeds, legends, rites or symbols, for though there is in the Christianity of the Church somewhat liturgical, legendary, ritual and symbolic, yet it is not essential to Christianity itself, and is to spirit-

ual men like you, no doubt, a help and not an incumbrance.
Now since all religion in general starts from the germs, and
primary essential truths of religion, which are innate with man;
since it is promoted by religious geniuses who, inspired by God,
appeal to these innate germs and truths, in man; since all religions are fundamentally the same, and only specific variations
of one and the same genus, and since, therefore, Christianity is
one religion among many, though it is the highest, and even a
perfect religion—it follows incontestably that Christianity also
must start from these same points. Accordingly we find history
verifying philosophy, for Christ always assumes these great
facts, viz. the existence of God, and man's sense of dependence
upon him, as facts given in man's nature. He attempted to excite
in man a more living consciousness of these truths, and to give
them a permanent influence on the whole character and life. His
words were attended to, just as the words of Homer or Socrates,
and the works of Phidias or Mozart were attended to. But ad-
miration for his character, and the influence of his doctrines, was
immeasurably greater than in their case, because he stood in
the very highest department of human interest, and spoke of
matters more concerning than poetry or philosophy, sculpture
or music. Now, if he assumed as already self-evident and un-
doubted, these two primary and essential truths of religion,
which had likewise been assumed by all his predecessors—and
if no miracle was needed to attest and give authority to his
doctrines respecting those very foundations and essentials of
religion, no man can consistently demand a miracle as a proof
that Christ spoke the truth when he taught doctrines of infinitely less importance, which were themselves unavoidable
conclusions from these two admitted truths. Gentlemen, I am
told by my minister, who is an argumentative man, it is a maxim
in logic, that what is true of the genus, is true also of the species.
If, therefore, the two fundamentals of religion, which in themselves involve all necessary subordinate truths thereof, be
assumed by Christ as self-evident, already acknowledged, and
therefore at no time, and least of all at that time, requiring a
miracle to substantiate them, I see not how it can be maintained,

that miracle was needed to establish inferior truths that necessarily followed from them. It would be absurd to suppose a miracle needed on the part of Socrates, to convince men that he uttered the truth, since no miracle could be a *direct* proof of that fact; and still more absurd would it be, while the most sublime doctrines, as soon as he affirmed them, were admitted as self-evident, to demand miraculous proofs for the truth of the legitimate and necessary deductions therefrom.

Still further, Gentlemen, Christianity is either the perfection of a religion whose germs and first truths are innate in the soul, or it is the perfection of a religion whose germs and first truths are not innate in the soul. If we take the latter alternative, I admit, that, following the common opinion, miracles would be necessary to establish the divine authority of the mediator of this religion; for devout men measuring the new doctrines by reason, conscience, and the religious sentiment— the only standard within their reach—and finding this doctrine contrary and repugnant thereto, must, of necessity, repel this religion, because it was unnatural, unsatisfactory, and useless to them. To open my meaning a little more fully by an illustration,—should a man present to my eyes a figure as the Ideal of Beauty, if that figure revolted my taste; were repugnant to my sense of harmony in outline, and symmetry of parts, I should say it could not be so; but if he had satisfactory credentials to convince me that he came direct from God, and to prove that this figure was indeed the Ideal of Beauty to the archangels, who had an aesthetic constitution more perfect than that of men, and therefore understood beauty better than I could do, I should admit the fact; but must, in that case, reject his Ideal Beauty, because it was the Ideal of Deformity, relatively, to my sense, inasmuch as it was repugnant to the first principles of human taste. Now if a religion whose germs and first truths are not innate in man, should be presented by a mediator furnished with credentials of his divine office, that are satisfactory to all men, the religion must yet be rejected. The religion must be made for man's religious nature, as much as the shoe must be made for the foot. God has laid the foundation of religion in man, and the religion

built up in man must correspond to that foundation, otherwise
it can be of no more use to him than St. Anthony's sermon was
to the fishes. There was nothing in the fishes to receives the
doctrine. But if we take the other alternative, and admit that
Christianity is the perfection of a religion whose germs and
first truths are innate in man, and confessed to be so, by him
who brings, and those who accept the religion, I see no need,
or even any use of miracles, to prove the authority of this mediator. To illustrate as before; if some one brings me an image,
as the Ideal of Beauty, and that image correspond to my idea
of the Beautiful, though it rise never so much above it, I ask no
external fact to convince me of the beauty of the image, or the
authority of him who brings it. I have all the evidence of its
excellent beauty that I need or wish for; all that is possible.
If Raphael had wrought miracles, his works would have had
no more value than now, for their value depends on no foreign
authority; but on their corresponding to ideal excellence.

But, besides, miracles in either alternative are exceedingly
weak arguments; yet if they have that constraining influence
some of you often claim for them, their authenticating power is
unlimited; and must, in all cases, constrain an eye-witness to
believe the miracle-worker is a divine messenger, and all his
words are truth. Now I will put a case: Suppose a miracle-
worker should assure a large audience in Boston, that it was a
moral duty to lie, steal, and kill; and, at their request, as proof
of his divinity, and the truth of his doctrines, should feed that
large audience to satiety, with a single loaf of bread; would they
believe the new doctrine in opposition to conscience, reason, and
religion? If they did thus believe, the fact would only prove
that their senses were more active than their souls; for, as things
visible are judged of by the eye, things to be tasted by the
palate, and things audible by the ear, just so what is addressed
to the spiritual powers, must be proved and accepted by the
spiritual powers, and not by the senses. To make my eye, ear,
or palate, evidence of the divinity of a man, or the truth of a
doctrine, is like setting the eye to judge sounds, and the ear
colors. In the case supposed, if men believe, their assent would

be forced, not voluntary, and therefore of no value, such a mediator must belittle his auditors before he can bless them. But if we take the accounts of the Bible, the most stupendous miracles of Moses and Jesus, had no influence to constrain belief, for their witnesses did not seem to know what a miracle could prove.

Gentlemen, I believe that Jesus, like other religious teachers, wrought miracles. I should come to this conclusion, even if the Evangelists did not claim them for him; nay, I should admit that his miracles would be more numerous and extraordinary, more benevolent in character and motive, than the miracles of his predecessors. This would naturally follow, if his power and obedience were more perfect than theirs. But I see not how a miracle proves a doctrine, and I even conjecture we do not value him for the miracles; but the miracles for him. I take it no one would think much of his common miracles, if they were not wrought by the God-man. The divine character of Christ gives value to the miracles, which cannot give divinity to Christ, or even prove it is there, as I take it; for many Christians believed Apollonius of Tyana wrought miracles, but they placed no value on them, because they had little respect for Apollonius of Tyana himself. The miracles of the Greek mythology, seem to have had no influence on the mind of the nation, because no great life lay at the bottom of these miracles. The same may be said of the miracles of the middle ages, and even of more modern times. We say these were not real miracles, and the saying is perhaps true, for the most part, but to such as believed them, they were just as good as true; yet their effect was trifling, because there was no great soul which worked these miracles. It may be said these differ in character from the Christian miracles, and the saying has its side of truth, if only the canonical miracles are included; but it is not true if the other miracles of Christian tradition are taken into account, for here malicious miracles are sometimes ascribed to him. But men found comfort in these stories only because they believed in the divinity of the character which lay at the bottom of the Christian movement.

Now, Gentlemen, if there are no *antecedent* objections to

Christ's possessing miraculous powers, there are some historical difficulties in the way of establishing *all* the miracles which he wrought. I allow there is a vein of the miraculous pervading human history; now and then it comes to light, perhaps even now-a-days. Without this admission, I cannot account for the almost universal belief, that miracles have been wrought, and especially by religious teachers. But it is a difficult matter to establish a particular miracle. A miracle, I suppose has two limits; the one is *the utmost verge of unassisted human ability,* the other is the *divine creative power,* which cannot, I reckon, be imparted to finite beings who have free-will. Now both of these limits are vague; exceedingly shadowy; it is perfectly impossible for me to fix them in speculation or practice. But since I can think of no more convenient limits, I will admit that all is a miracle which lies between these two extremes. But, as observations must not be made on the stars when pretty close to the horizon, I will be careful not to notice such acts as approach near the common powers of benevolent and cultivated men. A miracle, then, is a voluntary act, lying anywhere between these bounds, and if there is any meaning in the three words by which my old minister tells me miracles are called in the New Testament, they are fitted to excite *wonder,* to display unusual *power,* and are a *sign* of the character of the miracle-worker. Yet I take it they are not a proof the character is divine, for the serpent wrought the *first* miracle on record in the Bible, and Peter's shadow the *last,* I believe, not to mention Balaam's ass, the magicians in Egypt, and the exorcists in Christ's time, who had miraculous powers as Dr. Barnes thinks.

Gentlemen, I reckon it would be difficult to prove in a court of justice the reality of any one of the miracles ascribed to Jesus in the Gospels, with the exception of his resurrection, a miracle which he seems to have had no hand in bringing about; a miracle which was the corner stone of Paul's preaching, and of the Christian church. This, then, is not Christ's miracle, but God's act. There are several difficulties which hinder you from proving the reality of particular miracles.

1. There is the tendency to the marvellous in all ancient na-

tions, especially among the Jews, before and after the time of Christ. They never separated the true from the false; the common from the preternatural, I think; they did it least of all in the history of sacred persons. 2. The Epistles of the New Testament, though older than the Gospels, as you tell us, only mention the miracles in a general way; and but very rarely, only two or three times, at the outside, as I read it. They mention no particular miracles. If Paul had known Lazarus and two others were raised from the dead, would he have called Christ the "first fruits of them that slept"? He would rather, I reckon, mention these cases to prove a resurrection, and it is quite certain, if he had thought a belief in miracles so *necessary and essential,* he would have taken pains to spread the knowledge thereof in his Epistles, and would have charged Timothy to preach the miracles, as well as the crucifixion and resurrection. I take it a church might be Christian which believed only a single one of his ecclesiastical epistles, wherein no miracle, save the resurrection, is insisted on or mentioned. 3. The authority of the Evangelists is not quite satisfactory; not that they designed to tell what was false, for their sincerity is plain as the sun at noon-day—but they might be mistaken. Their inspiration did not free them from the notions of the age and nation; from wrong judgments, or their own temperaments. Gentlemen, one of your number, a scholar universally esteemed, whose talents and learning are respected, I doubt not, by his opponent in this controversy, has rejected several passages of the Gospels, as neither genuine nor authentic, and thinks, further, that some other passages are not strictly historical. I have read in some religious papers, that a German critic—Dr. Strauss I think—has explained a great deal of the New Testament into *Mythi,* as the papers called them, which had no foundation in fact. I do not like that Hebrew word, but thought long ago there was something legendary and romantic in the stories of Christ's birth, early life, and ascension to heaven. You would all admit this to one another, I reckon. Now these considerations would in some measure weaken the evidence of the Evangelists as to any one particular case of miracles, but would not detract from their moral character, or diminish the probability that Jesus worked miracles, though we cannot tell what they were. In saying this, I do not express any doubt on my own part of the *general* accuracy of their history of Christ, at least during his ministry.

Now, since these things are so, it seems to me much easier, more natural, and above all more true, to ground Christianity on the truth of its doctrines, and its sufficiency to satisfy all the moral and religious wants of man in the highest conceivable state, than to rest it on miracles, which, at best, could only be a sign, and not a proof of its excellence, and which, beside, do themselves require much more evidence to convince man of their truth, than Christianity requires without them. To me, the spiritual elevation of Jesus is a more convincing proof of his divinity, than the story of his miraculous transfiguration; and the words which he uttered, and the life which he lived, are more satisfactory evidence of his divine authority, than all his miracles, from the transformation of water into wine, to the resurrection of Lazarus. I take him to be the most perfect religious incarnation of God, without putting his birth on the same level with that of Hercules. I see the story of his supernatural conception, as a picture of the belief in the early Christian church, and find the divine character in the general instructions and heavenly life of Christ. I need no miracle to convince me that the sun shines, and just as little do I need a miracle to convince me of the divinity of Jesus and his doctrines, to which a miracle, as I look at it, can add just nothing. Even the miracle of the resurrection does not prove the immortality of the soul.

Gentlemen, I would say a word to that portion of your number who rest Christianity solely, or chiefly on the miracles. I would earnestly deprecate your theology. Happily, with the unlearned, like myself, this miracle-question is one of *theology,* and not of *religion,* which latter may, and does exist, under the most imperfect and vicious theology. But do you wish that we should rest our theology and religion—for you make it a religious question—on ground so insecure? on a basis which every scoffer may shake, if he cannot shake down—a basis which you acknowledge to be insecure when other religions claim to rest on it, and one from which your own teachers are continually separating fragments? To the mass of Christians, who are taught to repose their faith on miracles, those of the Old are as good as those of the New Testament, both of which are insecure. One of your number, a man not to be named without respect for his talents, his learning, and, above all, for his conscientious piety, a man whom it delights me to praise, though from afar— at one blow, of his Academic Lectures, fells to the ground all the most stupendous miracles of the Old Testament; and another, a party in this contest, has long ago removed several miracles from the text of the New Testament, and thrown discredit—unconsciously—upon the rest. If the groundwork of Christianity is thus to be left at the mercy of scoffers, or scholars and critics, who decide by principles that are often arbitrary, and must be uncertain, what are we the unlearned, who have little time for investigating such matters—and to whom Latin schools and colleges have not opened their hospitable doors— what are we to do? You tell us that we must not fall back on the germs and first truths of religion in the soul. You tell us that Christ *"established a relation between man and God, that could not otherwise exist,"* and the ONLY proof that this relation is *real,* and that he had authority to establish it, is found in the particular miracles he wrought, which miracles cannot, at this day, be *proved* real. Thus you repel us from the belief that the relation between God and man is founded in the nature of things, and was established at our creation, and that the authority of Christianity is not personal with Jesus, but rests on the eternal nature of Truth. Thus you make us rest our moral and religious faith, for time and eternity, on evidence too weak to be trusted in a trifling case that comes before a common court of justice. You make our religion depend entirely on something outside, on strange events which happened, it is said, two thousand years ago, of which we can never be certain, and on which yourselves often doubt, at least of the more and less. Gentlemen, we cannot be critics, but we would be Christians If you strike away a part of the Bible, and deny—what philosophy must deny—the perfect literal truth of the first chapter of Genesis, or the book of Jonah, or any part which claims to be literally true, and is not literally true, for us you have destroyed all value in miracles as evidence—exclusive and irrefragable— for the truth of Christianity. Gentlemen, with us, Christianity is not a thing of speculation, but a matter of life, and I beseech you, in behalf of numbers of my fellows, pious and unlearned as myself, to do one of two things, either to prove that the miraculous stories in the Bible are perfectly true, that is, that there is nothing fictitious or legendary from Genesis to Revelations, which yet professes to be historical, and that the authors of the Bible were never mistaken as to facts or judgments thereon; or leave us to ground our belief in Christianity on its truth,—which is obvious to every spiritual eye that is open,— on its fitness to satisfy our wants; on its power to regenerate and restore degraded and fallen man; on our faith in Christ, which depends not on his birth, or ascension; on his miraculous powers of healing, creating, or transforming; but on his words of truth and holiness; on his divine life; on the undisputed fact that he was ONE WITH GOD. Until you do one of these things, we shall mourn in our hearts, and repeat the old petition "God save Christianity from its friends, its enemies we care not for." You may give us your miracles, and tell us they are sufficient witness, but hungering and thirsting, we shall look unto Christ, and say, "Lord, to whom shall we go, Thou only hast the words of ever-lasting life," and we believe on Thee, for thy words and life proclaim themselves divine, and these no man can take from us.

I remain, Gentlemen,
with deep respect,
your affectionate servant,
LEVI BLODGETT

BIBLIOGRAPHY

Note: Bibliographies of Parker's works are available in the following studies:

John White Chadwick. Theodore Parker, a Biography. Boston and New York, Houghton Mifflin Co., 1900. Pp. xi–xx.
Charles W. Wendte, ed. Bibliography and Index to the Works of Theodore Parker. Boston, The Beacon Press, 1910. Pp. 11–50.
Henry Steele Commager. Theodore Parker, Yankee Crusader. Boston, Little, Brown, and Co., 1936. Pp. 311–331.

SOURCES FOR THE PRESENT STUDY

WORKS OF THEODORE PARKER

The Collected Works of Theodore Parker. 15 vols. Boston, The Beacon Press, 1907–1910.
This is the standard edition.
Levi Blodgett Letter. The Previous Question. Boston, Weeks, Jordan, and Co., 1840. Reprinted in full in the Appendix to the present volume, to which all citations refer.
West Roxbury Sermons 1837–1848. Boston, The American Unitarian Association, 1902.
These sermons are not included in *The Collected Works*.
A Critical and Historical Introduction to the Canonical Scriptures of the Old Testament. 2 vols. Boston, Charles C. Little and James Brown, 1843.
This was based on Wilhelm Martin Leberecht De Wette, *Lehrbuch der historisch-kritischen Einleitung in die kano-*

nischen und apocryphischen Bücher des Alten Testementes. Parker's work was much enlarged and included references to many German, English, and American works, many of which have been referred to in the notes of Chapter II of this study.

Review of David Friedrich Strauss, *Das Leben Jesu* (Tübingen, 1837), in the *Christian Examiner* (April, 1840).

Important, too, were Parker's and other's contributions in the field of higher criticism to such periodicals as the *Bibliotheca Sacra* (Andover), and the *American Biblical Repository* (Princeton and Andover), and the *North American Review* (Boston).

Letters to Convers Francis. A collection is in the possession of the Boston Public Library. Thirty-five of these letters were published in two early biographies. Some of the remaining forty-four are valuable as source material for a study of Parker's interest in Biblical criticism; several of these have been quoted in Chapter II of this work.

BIOGRAPHIES

John Weiss. Life and Correspondence of Theodore Parker. 2 vols. New York, D. Appleton and Co., 1864.

Octavius Brooks Frothingham. Theodore Parker, a Biography. New York, G. P. Putnam's Sons, 1874.

John White Chadwick. Theodore Parker, Preacher and Reformer. Boston, Houghton Mifflin Co., 1900.

Henry Steele Commager. Theodore Parker, Yankee Crusader. Boston, Little, Brown, and Co., 1936.

PARKER AND THE TRANSCENDENTALIST MOVEMENT

Blau, Joseph L., ed. American Philosophic Addresses, 1700–1900. New York, Columbia University Press, 1946. Pp. 659–663.

Bratton, Fred Gladstone. The Legacy of the Liberal Spirit. New York, Charles Scribner's Sons, 1943. Pp. 158–182.

Commager, Henry Steele. "The Dilemma of Theodore Parker,"

The New England Quarterly (June, 1933); and, "Theodore Parker, Intellectual Gourmand," *The American Scholar,* Vol. III (Summer, 1934).

The Dial. 4 vols. New York, 1844–1848.

Foster, Frank Hugh. A Genetic History of New England Theology. Chicago, The University of Chicago Press, 1907.

Frothingham, Octavius Brooks. Transcendentalism in New England. New York, G. P. Putnam's Sons, 1876. Pp. 302–321.

Goddard, Harold Clarke. Studies in New England Transcendentalism. New York, Columbia University Press, 1908.

Gohdes, Clarence L. F. The Periodicals of New England Transcendentalism. Durham, N.C., Duke University Press, 1931.

The Harbinger. 4 vols. New York, 1844–1848.

The Massachusetts Quarterly Review. 3 vols. Boston, 1847–1850.

Parrington, Vernon Louis. Main Currents in American Thought. New York, Harcourt, Brace and Co., 1939. Vol. II: The Romantic Revolution in America (1800–1860). The citations have been made from the one-volume edition.

Schneider, Herbert W. *A History of American Philosophy.* New York, Columbia University Press, 1946. Pp. 262–268.

———— "The Influence of Darwin and Spencer on American Philosophical Theology," *Journal of the History of Ideas,* VI (January, 1945), 3–18.

Wellek, René. "The Minor Transcendentalists and German Philosophy," The New England Quarterly, XV, 4, 1942.

Wells, Ronald Vale. Three Christian Transcendentalists. New York, Columbia University Press, 1943. This work, in general, contains many valuable suggestions toward a reinterpretation of the theological environment of Theodore Parker.

PARKER AND EMERSON

Cabot, James Elliot. A Memoir of Ralph Waldo Emerson. 2 vols. Boston, Houghton Mifflin Co., 1887.

Cameron, Kenneth Walter. Emerson the Essayist. 2 vols. Raleigh, N.C., The Thistle Press, 1945.

Chadwick, John White. Old and New Unitarian Belief. Boston, George H. Ellis, 1901.

Christian Examiner. Notably the volumes contemporary with the controversy.

Emerson, Ralph Waldo. Nature, Addresses, and Lectures. Boston, Houghton Mifflin Co., 1887.

———— The Divinity School Address. Boston, American Unitarian Association, 1839.

———— "Historic Notes on Life and Letters in New England." In *Lectures and Biographical Sketches*. Boston, Houghton Mifflin Co., 1887.

Emerson, Edward Waldo, and Waldo Emerson Forbes, eds. Journals of Ralph Waldo Emerson. Botson, Houghton Mifflin Co., 1910–1919.

Gray, Henry David. Emerson: a Statement of New England Transcendentalism as Expressed in the Philosophy of Its Chief Exponent. Palo Alto, California, Stanford University Press, 1917.

Mead, Edwin D. The Influence of Emerson. Boston, The Beacon Press, 1903. Chapter II is entitled "Emerson and Theodore Parker."

Newbrough, George F. "Reason and Understanding in the Works of Theodore Parker." *The South Atlantic Quarterly* (January, 1948).

Norton, Andrews. A Discourse on the Latest Form of Infidelity. Cambridge, John Owen, 1839.

Ripley, George. Letters on the Latest Form of Infidelity. Boston, James Munroe and Co., 1840.

INDEX

Affectional element, 91, 92
Agassiz, Louis J., 29
Aids to Reflection (Coleridge),
19
Alcott, Bronson, 4, 10, 11, 12, 13
American history, philosophy of
progress applied to, 116
Andover Theological Seminary,
60
Animism, 107

Bacon, Francis, 89, 90, 102, 104
Balfour, Walter, 59
Ballou, Hosea, quoted, 58
"Baltimore Sermon" (Channing),
57
Bancroft, George, 101
Baur, Ferdinand Christian, 47,
48, 53, 54, 131
Berkeley, George, 19
Bertholdt (Biblical scholar), 37,
38, 42, 46
Bible, study of, from viewpoint
of historical and literary criticism, 33-65, 130; essential aims
of criticism, 36; role of critic,
37; historical formation of the
canon, 37, 47; Parker a prophet
of historical criticism: a radical
in rejecting the claims of infallibility, 57, 63; viewpoints of
the more orthodox scholars,
57 ff.; authoritative view of,
60 f.; critical approach not generally welcomed, 62; attitude
toward errors in: acceptance of,

as an historical product, 63; aim
to destroy orthodox view of: bib-
liolatry Protestantism's most
flagrant sin, 64; conclusion re
Parker's Biblical scholarship,
65; rejection of argument for
Christian truth based on, 75,
159; not the finished document
of revelation, 120, 121; *see also*
Gospels
Biblical scholars, 33, 47, 57 ff.
Bleek (Biblical scholar), 38*n*
Boehme, Jacob, 4, 25*n*
Bradford, George, 13
Brownson, Orestes A., 4, 10, 12
Buckle, Henry Thomas, 102; Par-
ker's reliance on, 103

Cabot, Elliot, 13, 29, 31
Calvinism, degeneration, 112
Cameron, Kenneth Walter, 19
Canon, Biblical: study of histori-
cal formation, 37, 47
Carlyle, Thomas, 4, 10, 20, 87
Catholicism, degeneration, 112
Chadwick, John White, cited, 7-10
Channing, W. H., 12
Channing, William Ellery, 4, 11,
12, 13, 69; approach to Biblical
criticism: exposition of Unitar-
ianism, 57
Christ, *see* Jesus Christ
Christian Examiner, 13; excerpt,
56
Christianity, historical examina-
tion of the doctrines of its the-